DITCH

the

PITCH

DITCH *the* PITCH

The Art of Improvised Persuasion

STEVE YASTROW

SelectBooks, Inc.
New York

This first paperback edition of Ditch the Pitch™ is published by SelectBooks, Inc. For information address SelectBooks, Inc., New York, N.Y. 10003.

The Library of Congress has cataloged the hardbound edition published in 2014 by SelectBooks, Inc. as follows:

Library of Congress Cataloging-in-Publication Data
Yastrow, Steve, 1959-
Ditch the pitch : the art of improvised persuasion / Steve Yastrow. -- First edition.
    pages cm
 Summary: "Founder of business strategy consulting firm argues that customers are more persuaded by improvised conversations than scripted sales pitches. Presents techniques and practices for six habits people can learn to enable spontaneous conversations that persuade customers to say 'yes'"-- Provided by publisher.
 ISBN 978-1-59079-126-4
1. Selling--Psychological aspects. 2. Persuasion (Psychology) 3. Business communi-cation--Psychological aspects. I. Title.
 HF5438.8.P75Y37 2014
 658.8501'9--dc23
                    2013018384

Paperback Edition:
ISBN 978-1-59079-465-4

Interior book design and production by Janice Benight

Manufactured in the United States of America
10 9 8 7 6 5 4 3 2 1

CONTENTS

PART III
PUTTING DITCH THE PITCH
TO WORK   127

Part I

WHY DITCH THE PITCH

Sales pitches don't work.

When was the last time someone "convinced" you to do something?

When was the last time a hard sell worked on you?

When was the last time you enjoyed hearing someone's sales pitch?

Pitches don't work. Sales pitches, elevator pitches . . . all kinds of pitches. They just don't work. People don't want to hear sales pitches, and they are usually not persuaded by sales pitches. If you use a sales pitch to try to convince someone of something, and you manage to convince this person, you have succeeded in spite of your pitch, not because of it.

But the use of sales pitches is still the cornerstone of most persuasion, in our work lives and in our everyday lives. Even people who are not officially "salespeople" in their jobs tend to persuade through explanation, telling friends, family members, work colleagues, and customers why they should agree with them—just like a salesperson hawking his wares.

Sales pitches don't work. What should you do instead?

Ditch the Pitch.

The End of the Sales Pitch

Recently, a young salesperson was telling me about the training program in the large company where he had just been hired. The program extensively educated trainees about the product and the fundamentals of sales. He was preparing for his first milestone in the program: He would be evaluated by standing up in front of his mentors to deliver a pitch. Do we really think his ability to make a sales pitch is a good indicator of whether he will be able to persuade a skeptical customer to buy his products?

And on a more personal, everyday level, a friend recently told me how frustrated he was that he couldn't convince his wife that they should take a ski vacation this winter instead of their traditional Florida beach vacation. He replayed for me the highly logical argument he used as he tried to persuade his wife, counting off on his fingers all the compelling reasons they should go west to Colorado instead of south to Palm Beach. I'm not surprised he couldn't convince her. He sounded like a used-car salesman delivering a pitch.

This is typical of the way many of us try to persuade people. We become experts in our own arguments and rationales, and focus our communication efforts on convincing and cajoling. Salespeople go on sales calls armed with PowerPoint presentations, scripted agendas, and pre-conceived notions about what should happen on the call. (*"Mark, I'll start out by going over our bios, then you take them through the product line. After that, hand it back to me and I'll tell them about our new, innovative services."*) And the rest of us who aren't salespeople do things that are very similar as we try to persuade people, planning out what we're going to say, how we're going to say it, and why the other person *should* agree with us.

Here's a fact: You don't know what's going to happen in a situation requiring persuasion, so going in with a pre-scripted pitch will leave you less prepared, not more prepared.

So, what should you do?

Ditch the pitch.

Instead of relying on a pitch, improvise a fluid, made-in-the-moment conversation in which you are able to adapt what you say to the very specific things you learn in the conversation.

This book is about the end of the sales pitch, in both direct sales and other situations in which we have to persuade. It is about avoiding the inclination to pitch, and being able to identify when you slip into a pre-scripted pitch.

You can develop a persuasion style that is not based on pitches, but is based on relationship-building conversations that encourage people to agree with you and customers to do business with you.

No matter how accomplished a persuader you are, if you follow the Ditch the Pitch Habits described and presented in this book, you will acquire new talents that will help you go into persuasive conversations armed with confidence, rather than a sales pitch.

BUT I'M NOT A SALESPERSON

Okay . . . some readers are not salespeople. But unless you are an all-powerful leader of a sovereign kingdom, you continually need to persuade other people if you want to accomplish your own goals. No man is an island, and no person can exist without enlisting the cooperation of others. Ditch the Pitch Habits are not only lessons for salespeople; no matter what your job, they will help you become much more effective at getting people to agree with you.

DETECTING THE PITCH

Seven years ago, my brother Phil was diagnosed with multiple sclerosis. (Good news: As of this writing, he's in great shape. In fact, he he recently completed a marathon.) I remember those traumatic weeks after the initial diagnosis, which were filled with fear, uncertainty, and unanswerable questions. Choosing a course of treatment was one of the toughest things Phil faced in those first days. He was inundated with information from doctors, pharmaceutical companies, and experts. At one point he called me and said, "I've realized that all information about this disease falls into one of two categories: It either is or isn't a sales pitch." The easiest way for Phil to filter information was to discount all the sales pitches by focusing on information that was presented without a self-serving bias.

There is nothing more obvious than an overt sales pitch. And there is nothing more likely to awaken a customer's defenses.

What happens to you when you detect a sales pitch? Imagine these scenarios:

- You and your financial planner are discussing your long-term financial health, and you suddenly realize he is trying to sell you life insurance.

- You are chatting with someone at a party and you begin to think that he hopes to install the latest home security products in your house.

- A website that provides information about your disease is sponsored by a company that makes a medication your doctor didn't recommend.

- Your teenager comes to cuddle on the couch with you, telling you what a great parent you are, and then, as soon as you are lulled into a stupor of family happiness, asks you for money to buy a new computer.

Doesn't your perception change as soon as you detect the pitch?

WE ALL HAVE "CUSTOMERS"

If your job is in sales, it's obvious that the people you are trying to persuade are called "customers." But I encourage all of us, even those of us who are not salespeople, to think of the people we have to persuade as "customers."

A customer is anyone whose actions affect your desired outcomes.

At the most fundamental level, a customer is anyone whose actions affect your desired outcomes. We don't reach our goals on our own; we need the cooperation of others, and these people are our "customers." Have someone to persuade? That person is your customer.

By using this broad definition of the word "customer," you will be able to apply Ditch the Pitch Habits to every type of situation where you require persuasion to succeed.

WHY PITCHES DON'T WORK

In both our business and social lives, we do not want to be assaulted by one-way communication. We want to be invited into two-way conversations where we can be heard and understood.

But a "pitch" is inherently a one-way process. You pitch something over the side of a boat into the sea. A pitcher pours water in one direction—out. To throw a baseball is to pitch. What happens when a baseball pitcher throws a ball directly at a batter? The batter usually ducks or jumps out of the way, just like my brother did when he detected medical sales pitches related to managing his multiple sclerosis.

Let's explore why people are so averse to sales pitches.

Reason #1 why sales pitches don't work:
Your customer doesn't care about your story.

As Aristotle said, "the fool tells me his reasons. The wise man persuades me with my own."

Why is this so true?

I'm sorry to be the one to deliver the bad news, but here's the unadorned truth: Your customer doesn't really care what you have to say about yourself or about what you are trying to sell. Your story is not that interesting to him. He cares much more about his own story. This fact is at the heart of why sales pitches don't work.

Your customer spends a fraction of his time thinking about issues that are important to you, but he spends all his time living his own life. He only cares about your story to the extent that your story can impact his story. Consider these two approaches to a sales situation: "You like this car? Let me tell you about it," vs. "You like this car? Tell me what you like about it."

The greatest myth of marketing, sales, and persuasion is that other people want to hear our stories, and for this reason companies spend billions of dollars "getting the word out" with marketing communications and dumping sales pitches on people in sales calls. The truth is, customers care about their own stories, and a pitch is, inherently, the story of the seller. What do you think is more likely to catch the attention of your customer, a story about you or a story about him?

Reason #2 why sales pitches don't work:
If you are pitching, your customer will stop listening

Because your customer cares so much more about his own story than he cares about your story, it is really difficult to hold his attention as you deliver your pitch. If you give a pitch, it's highly likely that your customer will be distracted by thoughts of other things, everything from his next meeting to making sure he gets to his son's little league game tonight.

Your customer has many important things to do today. If you deliver a pitch as a monologue, those more immediate concerns will lure his attention away from you.

Reason #3 why sales pitches don't work:
Your customer wants to talk.

Your customer wants to talk. Specifically, your customer wants to talk about himself.

It is not enough to ask questions during your pitch or to leave moments in your pitch for your customer to talk. This won't feel like talking; it will feel like answering. It is the difference between a conversation and an interview.

Most people love to talk. And, they are much more engaged in the moment when they are talking than when they are listening. Especially when they are talking about themselves.

Reason #4 why sales pitches don't work:
It's a one in a million chance that your pre-scripted pitch
is what this particular customer wants or needs.

If you throw a pre-scripted pitch at someone, the odds of that message being the right message for that customer, at that particular time, are very slim.

Every customer has slightly different characteristics, needs, and interests, all of which can vary at any moment. A sales pitch is relatively inflexible, and will not be able to adapt to what a customer will reveal during the course of an interaction. And, if a customer doesn't know what he needs, a pitch doesn't give him a chance to discover it.

Most successful selling and persuasion isn't about convincing. It's about diagnosing. If you are pitching, it is only a coincidence if the pitch you toss at your customer lands in the right place. Unlike a sales pitch, a good persuasive conversation helps you identify the details that make this customer unique. And it helps you diagnose your customer's interests, needs, and opportunities.

If you are pitching, it is only a coincidence if the pitch you toss at your customer lands in the right place.

Reason #5 why sales pitches don't work: You make the customer do the work of attaching your features to his needs.

What you are offering may be exactly what your customer needs. But your customer has to see the connection between what you offer and what he needs. This isn't so easy.

If you are throwing a pitch at your customer, explaining how wonderful you are, and how your products or ideas benefit him, you are leaving it to your customer to bridge the connection between his specific needs and your offering. That's a lot of work, and he's not necessarily capable of or inclined to do it. Your approach to persuasion has to help your customer identify this connection.

Pitches are not interesting to customers. They don't hold customers' attention. They are not persuasive.

So what are we supposed to do? Stop selling and persuading? Of course not. We just have to stop making sales pitches and presentations. Instead, we must create persuasive conversations.

Replace Sales Pitches with Persuasive Conversations

2

Ditching the pitch is about jettisoning sales pitches and replacing them with persuasive conversations.

Real conversations are unscripted, unfolding in the moment. What each person says, at any point in time, is informed by what was said before. Genuine conversations are improvised. When you prepare for an interaction in which you have to sell something, stop thinking about what you want to say and start thinking about the kind of conversation you want to have.

A good conversation is also very collaborative. Think of the times when dialogue has led you and another person to ideas that neither of you would have thought of on your own. Neither of you viewed the conversation as if you were "talking to" the other person. You were "talking with" the other person.

Conversation is to our social lives what oxygen is to our physiological lives. We can't live without it. Genuine conversation is enriching; it makes us feel good, and it gives us energy. In contrast, what does it feel like when you have trouble conversing with someone? What does it feel like when someone dominates a conversation, reciting a monologue, never letting you get a word in? What does it feel like when someone tries to control the agenda in a conversation by forcing their topics on you, whether or not you want to talk about them? What does it feel like when you are speaking with someone and they are not giving you their full attention, stealing a glance around the room or down at their iPhone?

Conversation has served a valuable role in our evolution as social beings. As R.I.M. Dunbar writes in his essay "Language, Music, and Laughter: An Evolutionary Perspective," there is strong evidence that language evolved not just to help us communicate complex concepts to each other, but to support our need for social bonds. Non-human primates rely heavily on physical grooming to strengthen social bonds, with up to 20 percent of waking time devoted to grooming or being groomed.

Humans, with our larger brains, can maintain more social relationships than non-human primates—so many more that if we tried to use physical grooming to maintain these relationships, we would have to spend nearly half of our time stroking each other and combing each other's hair. That wouldn't leave much time for picking tubers out of the ground, slaying mastodons, or commuting into the city for work.

According to Dunbar, conversation, as a replacement for physical grooming, enables us to strengthen our social bonds while we are walking, feeding, foraging, or riding elevators, making it possible to maintain the numerous relationships enabled by our large human brains. In addition to serving important logistical needs in our lives, conversation also serves strong emotional needs.[1]

In his book *The Language Instinct,* scientist Steven Pinker describes how language evolved incrementally over human history, continually conferring a selective advantage on those with the best language skills. In each generation those individuals best equipped, through variation or mutation, to use language were more likely to survive and have offspring. As more generations passed and human language ability kept improving, the bar was continually raised, always favoring those with the highest-level, most cutting-edge language skills.[2]

Think about that for a second: In prehistoric human communities, the best conversationalists had the best chance of survival. Being able to talk, listen and respond was not just a "nice to have" trait. It was a trait that helped you live and pass on your genes. So you are all the proud descendants not only of the best hunters and gatherers, but of best of the best conversationalists.

When we *ditch the pitch,* we are not just employing good conversational hygiene. We are much more in tune with what it means to be human and to engage with other humans.

EARNING THE RIGHT TO BE HEARD

Imagine this: A salesperson launches into his pitch, confident that his message is exactly what his customer wants to hear.

Let's suppose for a moment that the message *is* just what the customer wants to hear. Does this mean the customer will hear it?

A customer may be standing in front of you, and may even be listening as you start speaking, but chances are that he is not actively listening to you. His doors to perception are not necessarily open to you. His attention may actually be pointed in another direction.

In our cacophonous world, where the average person is bombarded with about 5,000 marketing and sales messages each day, customers are generally not ready or eager to listen. The first thing you have to do if you want customers to listen to you, is to earn the right to be heard. Contrary to the most fundamental beliefs about sales, marketing, and persuasion, you do not earn the right to be heard just by delivering the right message to the right customer at the right time. You earn the right to be heard once you have engaged your customer in a dialogue that is meaningful to him.

To create a dialogue that a customer cares about, you must remember a key point we discussed above: Customers don't really care about our stories; they care about their own stories. At any moment you encounter a customer, that customer is in the middle of a rich personal narrative. The story that he really cares about is the story going on in his head, right now.

> *To earn the right to be heard, it is important to jump into your customer's world.*

The worst thing a persuader can do if he wants a customer to listen to him is to start to tell his own story. Not only does the customer not care about the persuader's story, the persuader is interrupting the rich story that the customer is currently thinking about.

To earn the right to be heard, it is important to jump into your customer's world. Don't force him to abandon his inner narrative. Discover what is going on with him, and try to become part of it.

Let's say you are a salesperson and today you are scheduled to have a meeting with a very important prospective customer. You have prepared extensively for this meeting, and you are certain that you know exactly what the customer would like to hear. As you greet each other and sit down in his conference room, the prospect sits back, as if he is ready to listen with rapt attention to your proposal.

Is he?

You must assume that he isn't.

Just because a customer looks like he is ready to listen, you should assume that he is not ready, and that you have to earn the right to be heard. He is in the middle of a very busy day, concerned about many other things, and it is possible that he has spent no time preparing for this meeting. If you jump right into telling your story, you are forcing him to jump straight out of his own day, right into yours.

Instead, use the first minutes of the meeting to enter his world. Engage him in a dialogue about himself. What is going on with him? What's important to him *right now*?

When you create a conversation that is centered on your customer, he will be much more comfortable and much more receptive. You are not interrupting his internal narrative, and you are focused on what he really cares about—his own world and his own situation. Once this happens, he will be much more open to listening to you.

A customer may be sitting right in front of you, making eye contact with you, but his ears may not be on. He may even think he is ready to listen, but his mind may be in another place. If you believe that you must earn the right to be heard during every moment you interact with customers, you will increase the chances that you actually will be heard.

Being heard by a customer is a privilege, not an entitlement. Keep earning that privilege, and you will find that you have also earned better customer relationships and better sales results.

This also applies directly to those of us who are not salespeople. If you are a plant manager talking to the CEO about a requisition of new equipment, or if you are the parent of a 13-year-old sitting down to a meeting with your rabbi in which you want to persuade him to let you host a hip hop-themed bar mitzvah party at the synagogue, you must assume that your customer is not ready to listen. In every case, you have to earn the right to be heard.

With this in mind, let's look at two different scenarios to explore the differences between sales pitches and sales conversations.

The Scene: A wedding planner meets with a bride and her mother. The bride is getting married next year and is thinking about hiring a wedding planner.

Scenario #1: The Sales Pitch

A wedding planner sits down with the bride and mother and launches into a description of her services, gushing about how a wedding is, "a girl's special day," and that she can help make the bride's wedding a dream come true. She shows them glossy brochures with pictures of weddings she has planned, emphasizing how each of her brides feel so special on her wedding day.

The bride interrupts, saying, "Actually, my fiancé is very excited about our wedding and wants to be involved in the planning. He couldn't make today's meeting because he had a work emergency. I told him we would update him on our meeting before we make any decisions."

"Well, that's great! It's good to let the boys think they are in charge," replies the planner with a wink. Then, she asks, "What venue have you chosen?" (The planner knows this is an easy way to assess the budget of a wedding because brides usually choose the venue first.)

The bride hasn't thought of the venue yet, and the planner doesn't quite know where to go from there. The bride is left with the distinct impression this planner has not heard a word she has said, and does not understand the couple's vision for the wedding.

Scenario #2: The Persuasive Conversation

The wedding planner sits down with the bride and her mother and says, "Let's talk about your wedding."

The bride gives the planner a description of colors and design themes she's been thinking about and mentions the need to accommodate out of town family. She mentions that her fiancé, a professional chef, wants to be involved in the planning. She also admits to confusion about where to have the wedding. "We just don't know how to get started choosing a venue. It's so overwhelming," she sighs. Her mother chimes in that her elderly mother will require special assistance and that they don't want anything outdoors.

From the wealth of information, the planner weaves a conversation in order to learn more about these issues, understand which is most important, and learn more about her customers. As the conversation unfolds, the planner realizes that the venue selection is the primary source of stress for the bride. She assures them she will limit the selections based on their preferences and budget and can handle the negotiation with the venue management. She also learns that the groom's primary interest is participating in the catering decisions, and they schedule a meeting that can include the groom to discuss the options.

The bride and her mother leave this meeting feeling reassured that the wedding planner understands them and are confident the wedding will be stress-free if they hire her.

I experienced a similar contrast one afternoon recently when my wife, Arna, and I shopped for a new car. We were pretty sure which car we wanted to buy. When we arrived at the dealership, thinking we were going to leave with a new car, the salesperson, Deborah, launched into a description of the car's features, listing her points as she spoke by tapping the index finger of her right hand on the fingers of her left hand. When she finished telling us about the car's gas mileage, safety ratings, and cup holders she stopped and looked at us, as if she was waiting for us to say, "Great, we'll take one!"

When I asked if we could test-drive the car, Deborah seemed a bit put-out and then went to arrange it. Once we were seated in the car, Arna asked Deborah about one of the sections of the dashboard. From her seat in the back, Deborah answered Arna by giving us a description of *all* the features on the dashboard, covering each quickly. Then she settled back in her seat and directed us to the route that she routinely takes customers on for test drives. Deborah never asked us any questions and never learned anything about us, and, as a result, never addressed any of our interests or concerns. When we returned to the dealership, she recounted the features of the car and wound up her pitch by asking if we wanted to go back to her desk to write-up a contract. She seemed genuinely surprised when my wife and I declined and said we wanted to think about it.

We had entered the dealership thinking we wanted to buy this car, but we left confused about whether this was the right car for us. Instead of helping us make a decision that was right for us, all Deborah did was provide information that was readily available in a brochure.

Then we drove to another dealership where we met a salesperson named Jessica. She began a conversation with us, in which she learned that we were shopping for a sedan for Arna to replace the van she'd been driving while our children were young. Through the conversation, Jessica learned that Arna was interested in a hybrid with high gas mileage and that we tend to buy and keep our cars for eight or nine years. Jessica showed us the hybrid in the showroom and asked if we'd like to drive this model. While the attendant retrieved a car for us to drive, we continued talking about our family, the weekend driving trips we take to Michigan, and the other cars we were thinking about.

Once in the car, with Arna in the driver's seat, Jessica patiently walked her through the workings of the car. As they covered each of the car's features, Jessica never recited all the information we could have readily found in a brochure. Instead, she let Arna's interests and questions guide the discussion. A real conversation emerged, and it became clear how each of the features of the car could meet our needs.

Jessica then asked us what kind of driving we'd like to do to test-drive the car and suggested a route that included highway and residential neighborhoods. As we drove the car and continued talking with Jessica, we began to see ourselves owning this car in a way that we didn't experience at the first dealership. While the first salesperson had told us about the car she was selling, Jessica engaged us in a conversation about what was important to us. She didn't talk about the car. She talked about Arna and Steve.

Jessica's persuasive conversation took longer than Deborah's sales pitch. But Jessica's investment was well worth it. She earned a commission and began a relationship that could lead to future business and referrals.

Human beings are wired for conversation, not for hearing pitches. For this reason, we are more receptive when we are engaged in a two-way conversation than when we are hearing a one-way monologue.

GOOD PERSUASIVE CONVERSATIONS ARE DIAGNOSTIC

Imagine this scenario: You are sitting in an exam room at your doctor's office. Your doctor walks in, says hello, hands you a piece of paper, and says, "Here's a prescription for what ails you."

"Doctor," you say, "how do you know how to treat me if you haven't asked me any questions about how I feel?"

"I have notes right here," he answers, "from our receptionist. It says that when you called for your appointment you said you have a stomachache. This medicine is how I treat stomachaches."

Clearly, this situation is absurd. No doctor would prescribe a treatment before interviewing and examining his patient. No doctor would assume upon his first contact with a patient that he knows exactly what kind of stomachache this patient has.

So why are millions of salespeople doing this same thing, at this very minute, all over the world? Why are salespeople walking into meetings with customers and delivering pre-written pitches? Why are salespeople wasting chance encounters with prospects by delivering pre-scripted "elevator pitches?" Isn't it just as absurd for a salesperson to walk into a room and start prescribing solutions as it is for a doctor? How in the world do you know what kind of stomachache your customer has before you ask her?

Similarly, in non-sales situations, isn't it absurd to pre-suppose how to persuade someone before you have a chance to converse with them? To assume you know and understand their thoughts or concerns before they tell you what they are?

Don't prescribe before you diagnose. A persuasive conversation should be diagnostic, not prescriptive.

Let's break down the differences between a sales pitch and a persuasive conversation.

Sales Pitch vs. Persuasive Conversation

The Sales Pitch	*The Persuasive Conversation*
You deliver it	You and your customer engage in it
It's about you	It's about the customer
You script it, planning what to say ahead of time	You and your customer create it, determining what to say as the conversation unfolds
It is prescriptive	It is diagnostic
It is one-way	It is two-way
You sell to your customer	You help your customer buy
You guess about what you should say	Your customer leads you to what to say
You wait for feedback	You receive feedback throughout
You sell to a customer	You build a relationship
You talk about what you are selling	You talk about your customer
It is boring to your customer, and it gets more boring as it proceeds	It is interesting to your customer, and it gets more interesting as it proceeds
It's a coincidence if you say what your customer wants to hear	You are very likely to say what your customer wants to hear
There's a one in a million chance it is appropriate to your customer's situation.	It's highly likely to be appropriate to your customer's situation.
It is relatively quick	It takes an investment of time

IMPROVISATION: THE KEY TO CREATING AUTHENTIC PERSUASIVE CONVERSATIONS

By their very nature, persuasive conversations must be fluid, spontaneous, and fresh. When customers feel as if they are experiencing something that is being created new, on the spot, they are much more likely to be engaged by it than by a pre-written script. After all, if we were in the same room talking together, what would seem more important to you, something I wrote in a PowerPoint presentation yesterday or something we discovered together through conversation, right now?

Great persuasive conversations are improvised. Let's take a look at the concept of improvisation and how it can help you become a more effective persuader.

Improvisation Creates Persuasive Conversations

3

By definition, improvisational acting means working without a script with scene partners to create something out of nothing, in the moment.[3]

—TOM YORTON
CEO, Second City Communications

What audiences love about improvisation is that they discover things as the actors discover them. There's that moment where the audience members feel like they are playing along.[4]

—ANNE LIBERA
Director of Comedy Studies at Second City
Author of *The Second City Almanac of Improvisation*

Improvisation is the art of not knowing what you're going to do or say next, and being completely okay with that.[5]

—MICK NAPIER
Founder, Annoyance Theater
Author of *Improvise*

Improvisation has been part of my life for a long time. I've been improvising on guitar since my teenage years, and my favorite music to hear live is either jazz or rock performances featuring a lot of improvisation. I enjoy improvisational stage performances, and so it is fortunate that I live in Chicago, the undisputed stage improvisation capital of the world and the home of Second City, iO, The Annoyance and many other improv theaters. While writing *Ditch the Pitch,* I interviewed many improvising actors and musicians, and will use their wisdom throughout this book to shed light on ways that you improve your ability to persuade through improvisation.

This book's central theme is that improvisation is one of the most important tools you can use to improve your performance

••••••••••••••••••••

To sell effectively, you must acquire the ability to work without a script.

••••••••••••••••••••

as a persuader, whether your job is focused specifically on sales or if your work requires other types of persuasion. To persuade effectively, you must acquire the ability to work without a script. You have to develop the fluency to adjust to the nuances of the moment and the flexibility to adapt to whatever situation you find yourself in with your customer. You must learn to improvise.

The good news: You *can* learn to improvise, using the tools that musicians and actors use. And, even better, you were born to improvise.

HUMANS WERE BORN TO IMPROVISE

We are, at our core, improvisational beings. In fact, **improvisation is one of the most natural things we do. You are already an awesome improviser.**

In his book, *Our Inner Ape,* noted primatologist Frans de Waal focuses on humanity's two closest relatives, chimpanzees, and bonobos. Humans, chimps, and bonobos all share nearly 99 percent of their DNA. Here's a passage from *Our Inner Ape* that describes how these species' behavior is not pre-programmed, and that we use improvisation to navigate the numerous situations they encounter every day:

It is undeniable that we have inborn predispositions, yet I don't see us as blind actors carrying out nature's genetic programs. **I see us rather as improvisers** who flexibly adjust to other improvisers on the scene with our genes offering hints and suggestions.

Chimps, bonobos, and humans all spend years growing up in their communities, learning how the world works, learning how to interact with other members of their community, learning how to thrive . . . in essence, learning to improvise.

> Our lives are not pre-programmed, and our actions are not hard-wired. We encounter brand new situations every day, and our success depends on our ability to improvise.[6]

The world is always throwing unexpected information and situations at human beings and our primate cousins. If we conduct our lives in a rigid, pre-programmed way, we will continually collide with the world around us. But most of us don't approach the world this way. We improvise.

Douglas Ewart is a creative musician, in addition to being a professor at the School of the Art Institute of Chicago. His ensemble, Douglas Ewart and the Inventions, plays completely improvised concerts with no prior conversation among the players about what they are going to play. When I interviewed Douglas, the first thing he said was, "Improvisation is a daily activity. Crossing the street requires improvisation. Even when you cross with the light, you have to be alert, and you have to judge if the person driving a car is being mindful of you. If not, you have to adjust. You improvise."[7] When Douglas Ewart and the Inventions improvise an entire concert, they are not only displaying master musicianship, they are expressing, in a virtuosic way, one of our most natural human abilities.

● ● ● ● ● ● ● ● ● ● ● ● ● ● ● ● ● ● ● ●
You are already an awesome improviser.
● ● ● ● ● ● ● ● ● ● ● ● ● ● ● ● ● ● ● ●

R.I.M. Dunbar, the anthropologist who believes that conversation is not only for transmitting information but for solidifying our social bonds, also posits that humans used music as a social "glue" for more than a million years before full language developed. Imagine families of *homo erectus* or *homo neanderthalensis* sitting around their campfires hundreds of thousands of years ago, chanting. They certainly weren't reading from printed music! They most certainly developed their traditional chants and songs the way much folk music has been created in the last thousand years: through improvisation. Listening to each other, imitating each other, embellishing the sounds of others through nightly improv sessions, they created the songs that distinguished their particular community. Our ancestors spent a million years improvising before they ever even had the idea of writing down their music.

Douglas Ewart's point and the ideas described by Frans de Waal and R.I.M. Dunbar are essentially the same: your life, even your business life, is filled, each day, with novel situations. You will not be able to navigate those situations unless you are able to see each one as a unique, one-of-a-kind situation, and respond in a unique, one-of-a-kind way. Fortunately, improvisation is one of the most natural things we do.

One of the most common places we improvise in our conversations with others. In *The Lanuguage Instinct,* Steven Pinker references a principle brought forth by linguist Noam Chomsky: "Virtually every sentence that a person utters or understands is a brand-new combination of words, appearing for the first time in the history of the universe." Using language is not a set of pre-programmed responses to external stimuli, it is a highly-advanced capability to improvise something new every time we speak, to understand these new things when others say them, and to improvise an instant response to what we hear.

Mick Napier, founder of Chicago's Annoyance Theater, says, "I have been teaching improvisation for twenty-five years, and what am I doing? I'm teaching people to say that which they didn't know they were going to say before right now, which is what everyone does, all the time."

Mick adds, "I'll bet you that if someone who sells cars is having a drink with a friend and is describing the cars he sells, it will be much better and more persuasive than a sales pitch he's memorized." We improvise our conversations when we are with our friends, and this natural method of communication is much more authentic and effective than pre-scripted pitches.

Mick's point is pretty ironic: The salesperson is less effective as a persuader when he is selling a car than when he is having a drink with a friend, because a pitch is not as natural as a spontaneous conversation. When I asked John Moulder, one of today's top improvising jazz guitarists, what first comes to mind when he thinks of improvisation, John immediately answered, "Improvisation asks people to be genuine and true to themselves, with honesty about what they are doing. That's the best thing about improvisation when it happens—it's true self expression."[8]

In 1959, The Second City comedy club and theater was founded in Chicago and went on to become one of the most influential names in improvisational comedy. The Second City has served as the training ground for Tina Fey, Steve Carrell, Stephen Colbert, Jim and John Belushi, Bill Murray, Dan Aykroyd, and Martin Short, to name only a few. No other organization is associated with improvisational acting in the way Second City is, and most improv theaters in the United States can, in some way, trace their "genealogy" to Second City.

Stage improv presents us with a very instructive model for ditching the pitch. Actors improvising a scene on stage engage their audience by creating a fresh, spontaneous story, a story that emerges as the scene unfolds, without preconceived notions and based on the interchanges between the actors and the reactions of the audience.

Tom Yorton, of Second City Communications says, "Good improvisation is all about listening, reacting in the moment, creating, and supporting the ideas of others."[9] This is exactly what has to happen in a persuasive conversation.

An improvising actor will fail if he insists on a particular path for a scene. If he has preconceived notions for what he wants to say and what should happen, he will most likely kill the scene. On the other hand, if he is alert, aware, and flexible, he will be able to adapt to whatever his stage partners say and do, and together they will create a scene that engages the audience. He can have a general idea of what might happen, and can have a suite of tools and ideas in his mind, but he can only use the ideas and tools that are suggested by the unfolding scene.

The popular TV show *Whose Line Is It Anyway?* is a great example of stage improvisation. In this show, actors create ideas that they never could have conjured if they had sat down, pencils in hand, to write the scene as a script. There is a magic of the moment, a creativity born of spontaneity, that emerges if improvising actors embrace alertness and flexibility.

Unfortunately, most salespeople don't employ the flexibility of stage improvisers. They focus on what they want to say and work hard to get each point of their sales pitch into a sales call. Imagine if a salesperson were to abandon the idea that a sales call is a chance to deliver his story, and, instead, embraced the ideas of stage improvisation as a way to engage his customer in a collaborative dialogue. As Tom Yorton says, "Improv creates an environment where new and bolder ideas are offered and refined quickly."[10] Without consciously realizing it, the salesperson's customer would become a willing actor in the newly evolving scene, participating collaboratively to create these new, bold ideas.

Mick Napier offers this insight: "Improvisation is the art of not knowing what you're going to do or say next and being completely okay with that." That "okayness" is hard for a lot of people.

> ●●●●●●●●●●●●●●●●●●●●●
> *Improvisation is the art of not knowing what you are going to do or say next, and being completely okay with that.*
> —MICK NAPIER
> ●●●●●●●●●●●●●●●●●●●●●

It is essential to develop the "okayness" Mick is talking about, and even to go beyond being "completely okay" with improvisation, *relishing* the opportunities that come by abandoning pre-written scripts.

Music producer Yossi Fine, who has produced many successful records in the United States, Israel, and Africa, in addition to being an outstanding musician in his own right, is one of those people who relishes the opportunities that beg for improvisation. "Sometimes, in a recording session, when things don't go exactly as planned, I look at it as a great chance to improvise and be creative," says Yossi. "First, I tell myself that I will know what to do. Once you say 'I know what to do,' you *will* know what to do."[11]

As Mick Napier adds, "When you can get away from 'that which you once created' you open yourself up to infinite possibilities." If you do this, Mick explains, you leave yourself space to create the right thing for the right moment. "I've seen people begin to flourish," Mick explains, "as a result of that breakthrough where you aren't attempting to reproduce that which you once created, but you're creating everything anew."

Be okay with spontaneity, and the world opens up to you.

Tom Yorton adds, "At its essence, improvisation is about affirmation, creation, and mutual support."[12] Improvisation is the ultimate collaboration. The most universal principle of stage improvisation is called "Yes, and . . .," a very simple, yet powerfully effective idea. Here's how it works: Imagine two actors are on a stage, improvising a scene in a doctor's waiting room, when one of them says, "I've never seen a doctor's office with dandelions growing out of the carpet." If the other actor says, "There are no dandelions growing out of this carpet," the scene dies. But if the second actor says, "**Yes**, Dr. Jones is so busy he can't keep up with pulling weeds. **And** look at the size of that caterpillar climbing the wall!" the scene will move forward.

No matter what another person says on stage, you never say "no." You agree with what they offer you. You never resist or deny, because resistance and denial will ruin the scene. You always agree with what the other person offers by saying "yes," following it with "and" to move the scene forward.

How to use the principle of "Yes, and . . ." will be discussed more fully later in this book when we discuss specific habits that can help you use the tools of improvisation to improve your persuasive conversations. What we will see is that mutual agreement between you and your customer will propel a persuasive conversation forward the way mutual agreement moves an improvised scene forward at Second City.

Don't worry . . . you don't have to be funny

The Second City method also teaches that improvisation skills are not intrinsically about being funny. Humor is a byproduct of the listening, spontaneity and mutual support on which improvisation is based. This humor helps engage the improv actors' audience. A salesperson can use the principles of improvisation to engage customers and improve his sales results without ever cracking a joke.

Humor is only one of the possible outcomes of improvisation. Improvisation is, first and foremost, about navigating our wild, unpredictable world. Stage actors use improv to get laughs, while jazz musicians use improvisation to communicate feelings with sound. Emergency room nurses use improvisation to deal with crises, applying years of learning to the one-of-a-kind trauma they are treating. NFL quarterbacks use improvisation when they see an unexpected defense, drawing on hours of practice to call an "audible" and adapt to the new situation. Chimpanzees improvise to negotiate the sharing of food with members of their group. You don't have to be funny to be an amazing improviser. You can use improvisation to persuade others effectively.

But what if I fail?

If an actor misses a line or a cue in a scripted play, it can cause the scene to grind to a screeching halt. But it's not possible for an actor to miss a line or a cue in an improvised scene because what happens next is not pre-determined.

It's not possible for you to fail when you improvise; an idea or comment that seems like a mistake becomes a segue to the next part of your conversation. Later we will learn concepts, such as *every idea is a bridge to the best idea*, and how to *make accidents work*, that will help you understand how you can always a move a persuasive conversation forward, no matter what happens.

Not worrying about failure helps improvising actors—and great salespeople—to take the risk of improvising without knowing what might come next. "Improvising can be spectacularly successful, and more exhilarating, hilarious, and joyful than working off a script," says Tom Yorton. "Actors do it because there is something very special about risking with other actors to create something completely original, something that will never be replicated exactly again."

As I will describe in later chapters, creating "something completely original, something that will never be replicated exactly again" is a key ingredient of a successful persuasive conversation.

WHAT IS IMPROVISATION?

Mick Napier's precept that improvisation is "not knowing what you are going to do or say next, and being totally okay with that" implies much about improvisation. How else can we describe improvisation?

Improvisation is freedom. Improvisation frees you from the constraints of a pre-determined story. It also frees you from pre-determined expectations that can only disappoint you, since things rarely turn out exactly as you think they will.

Improvisation is exciting. Improvisation is exciting because anything might happen next. When you improvise, you are open, ready and confident to adapt your conversation to an evolving situation. And improvisation is exciting for your customer too, because she feels like a participant, not an observer.

Improvisation is natural. We are born to improvise. We evolved to improvise so that we will always be prepared to adapt to the ever-changing world we live in. Improvisation is in our genes.

Improvisation is flexible. Improvisation is flexible, allowing you to adjust your story to make it optimally and maximally relevant to your customer. You hear her and you see her, you adapt to her, making the story more significant for her.

> *Improvisation can never be stale because it hasn't had time to get stale.*

Improvisation is fresh. When improvisation happens, it's fresh like a pie that just came out of the oven, steam rising from the top. Improvisation can never be stale because it hasn't had time to get stale. It has a palpable freshness.

Improvisation is affirmative. It's affirmative because you're always saying "yes," agreeing to go with the flow, and never resisting.

Improvisation is collaborative. Sure, it's possible to improvise a monologue, but it's much more interesting to improvise a dialogue.

How do they do that?

Whenever I am watching great stage improvisation with friends, someone will say, inevitably, *"How do they do that?"* In fact, I think it is nearly impossible for someone to watch the TV show *Whose Line Is It Anyway?* for the first time and not ask that question. Instead, what you should be asking is, *"How can I do that?"* And that's what *ditching the pitch* is about. The purpose of the Ditch the Pitch Habits is to help you create spontaneous conversations and become a much more effective persuader.

Great stage improvisers are able to invent their material in a split second. They respond perfectly to what their stage partners say, and they make it look effortless. A great salesperson behaves similarly during a persuasive conversation. He reacts perfectly to everything his customer says, improvising responses without being bound to a script. Effortlessly, he navigates the conversation, keeping his customer engaged. He works with the fluency and agility of an improvising stage actor.

Many people imagine that the stage improviser is just quick-witted, or he was just "born funny," and that the great salesperson is also just quick-witted, or she is a "natural-born salesperson." But that's not why these people succeed.

They succeed because they have learned the techniques of improvisation, techniques that free them from scripts and sales pitches. The same can be said about musical improvisers. Jazz or rock players who meet each other for the first time can begin improvising together immediately, not because they are practitioners of ESP, but because they have learned tools that help them express their natural-born human ability to improvise.

Developing your ability to improvise is really not that difficult, as long as you follow the advice and habits that I will describe in upcoming sections. You don't need to be funny, or quick-witted, or charismatic. What really counts is practicing the simple, straightforward habits of improvisation in your everyday persuasive conversations. In the next section I will show you how to use improvisational tools to *ditch the pitch*.

Part II

THE DITCH THE PITCH HABITS

When I conduct workshops, I frequently ask audiences to describe what habits are. People are very clear about the word "habit" and I always hear some version of: "It's something you do often without having to think about it."

Habits influence many of the actions we take, but they are not pre-scripted, hard-wired behaviors. The habit of looking both ways before you cross the street helps you get to the other side, whether you are crossing a busy Manhattan street at rush hour or a small-town street at dusk. The habit of putting your fork down once you are full will help you avoid overeating at any dining occasion.

Habits are essential for improvisation, because they provide us with frameworks for understanding the novel situations we encounter and for helping us craft spontaneous responses to those situations. When you develop Ditch the Pitch Habits, you will be able to improvise customer encounters, no matter who the customer is or what the situation is.

In this section, we are going to explore six Ditch the Pitch Habits:

- In Chapter Four we will learn how to *Think input before output* and to *Size up the scene.*

- In Chapter Five, I will describe how to *Create a series of yeses* and to *Explore and heighten.*

- Chapter Six will include habits *Focus the conversation on your customer* and *Don't rush the story.*

Actions become habits only after much practice. To help you develop Ditch the Pitch Habits, I will introduce a number of practices that you can integrate into your daily customer encounters, in order to create good habits that will help you *ditch the pitch*. By repeatedly using practices, you will find that the habits will quickly become second nature.

For reference, I suggest you mark these pages and refer to the chart on page page 33 frequently as you are learning the Ditch the Pitch Habits:

Don't worry. You don't have to work on these habits all at once. As with any good habit, these habits can be developed over time. As you work on them, your ability to *ditch the pitch* will improve and you will see improvements in your performance as a persuader.

THE DITCH THE PITCH HABITS

Chapter 4: Figure Out What's Going On

HABIT #1
Think input before output

- Practice: Be alert
- Practice: Say less to notice more
- Practice: Turn down your analytic brain

HABIT #2
Size up the scene

- Practice: Know who you are with
- Practice: Understand the context of your conversation
- Practice: Listen for the game

Chapter 5: Go with the Flow

HABIT #3
Create a series of "yeses"

- Practice: Say, "Yes, and . . ."
- Practice: Work with what you are given
- Practice: Ensure your customer keeps saying yes

HABIT #4
Explore and heighten

- Practice: Find your customer's path
- Practice: Get rid of your but
- Practice: Make accidents work

Chapter 6: Let a Shared Story Emerge through Your Conversation

HABIT #5
Focus the conversation on your customer

- Practice: Make 95% of the conversation about your customer
- Practice: Obey the one-paragraph rule
- Practice: Weave your stories together

HABIT #6
Don't rush the story

- Practice: Don't load the slingshot
- Practice: Leave things in your pocket
- Practice: Create callbacks

Suggestion: mark this page and refer back to this chart as you read chapters 4, 5, and 6.

Figure Out
What's Going On

HOW TO START A PERSUASIVE CONVERSATION

When you first enter into a persuasive conversation, you don't know what's going on.

Even if you've known your customer for a long time, and especially if you haven't, you can't possibly know what your customer is thinking or the nuances of his mood, interests, and needs. You also don't know the details of his situation. Even if you are with a customer with whom you speak every day, you can't assume that you know what's happened since yesterday.

The first thing you have to do when you enter into a persuasive conversation is figure out *"What's going on here?"* Let's explore the first Ditch the Pitch Habit that will help you *Figure out what's going on* in a persuasive conversation.

HABIT #1
Think Input Before Output

SCENE: You are a salesperson in a conversation with a top sales prospect. After months of courting him, he is finally opening up and sharing information about his business with you. While your prospect is talking you feel your phone vibrate in your jacket pocket. "Who could it be?" you wonder. "Oh no, I forgot to call Fred back," you realize, deciding that you'll have to call Fred as soon as this meeting is over. You mentally rehearse what you will say to Fred when you call him to apologize for not calling sooner.

Suddenly you hear your prospective customer say, "Yeah, that's one of the most important things we need to worry about these days, and anybody who could help us with it would be worth their weight in gold. Can you?" You have no idea what he was talking about, and now you have no idea what to say.

The best improvisers are the best listeners. Whether it's Douglas Ewart and the Inventions playing a completely improvised concert at the Velvet Lounge on Chicago's south side, the improv actors performing nightly on numerous Chicago stages, or an accomplished salesperson *ditching the pitch*, improvisation is an "ears first" exercise; great improvisers focus on input before output. Every scene in a well-done stage improv performance is also a showcase of attention and listening. Whenever I watch a successful improv scene at The Second City, Chicago's Annoyance Theater or any other improv venue, I am as much amazed by what the actors notice as by what they say and do. As Susan Messing, one of Chicago's most talented—and popular—improvisational actors says, "The best way to be prepared for an improv scene is to be awake and alert."[13]

The same thing is true in persuasive conversations. If you are paying attention, the ideas will come to you. Attention, alertness, and awareness provide the fuel for spontaneous ideas.

The key is to *Think input before output,* noticing the information available to you before you determine your response, and using that information to help you have a fresh, spontaneous persuasive conversation.

🌀 PRACTICE: Be Alert

Did you ever notice how some people are really quick on their feet? They always know exactly what to say, whether they are having fun at a party, fielding tough questions in a business meeting, or improvising on a stage. They react quickly, but it never seems forced or nervous. It always feels natural.

What's their secret?

One of the best ways to be quick on your feet is to *Be alert, Thinking input before output.* As *The Second City Almanac of Improvisation* says, "Everything each character does or says should affect the other characters onstage."[14] Jessica Rogers, a Chicago improv actor and instructor at the Second City Training Center says, "You must be open to all new pieces of information." Every new piece of information has the possibility of influencing the scene, so the actors don't want to miss anything.

I asked Charna Halpern, the founder of the iO theaters in Chicago and Los Angeles (formerly ImprovOlympic), what makes for great improvisation. The first thing she said, without hesitation, is, "The ability to really listen, actively listen, and build on each other's ideas." Notice that Charna didn't say that being funny, clever or witty is the key to being a great improviser. She said it is most important to first focus on *input*, to take in what's going on around you, rather than *output*, what you want to say.

Charna's company does a lot of work in the business world, training people to use improv techniques on the job. "We find in the corporate world that a lot of people are just impatiently waiting to speak. They're not really listening, they are just thinking ahead to what they want to say." Is it any wonder that communication in companies is often so poor?

Being alert is, not surprisingly, also the secret to a persuader being quick on her feet. It's not that she is wittier or smarter than other people; it's that she notices the nuances of what her customers say and considers every relevant piece of information happening in her environment. This gives her a wider range of options for adapting specifically to the conversation.

> *The key to being quick on your feet isn't in your feet, or on your lips. It's in your eyes and ears.*

The key to being quick on your feet isn't in your feet, or on your lips. It's in your eyes and ears. *Being alert*, by listening and observing, is the first rule of improvisation. *Think input before output*, and you'll be surprised at the amazing things you are able to say.

"The next message you need is always right where you are."
—RAM DASS

Improvisation happens in the "now." Alertness to the present moment triggers responses, so the first step to *ditching the pitch* and creating effective persuasive conversations is to "notice the now."

Watch a stage actor improvising or a winning quarterback dropping back into the pocket after taking the snap, and what you will notice is someone who is completely tuned in to the present moment. Nothing else is going on for this person but what is happening right now. This enables him to be so alert that he can pick up all sorts of important details. If his mind wanders for even a split second, his scene could die or he could throw an interception.

Watching Susan Messing perform (or even just having a conversation with her) treats you to a virtuosic performance of "working with the now." When I spoke with Susan about how she approaches improvisation, she says, "I focus on what is right in front of me," and her performances support this.

Contrast this with a story Charna Halpern told me about a radio interview she and Mike Myers did on the 25th anniversary of the iO theaters. "Mike had had a series of travel complications making it in for the interview, which actually made for a very funny story—especially the way Mike told it. When the interview started, the radio show host said, 'Charna Halpern and Mike Myers, I'm so glad you could make it today.' Mike answered with, 'Well, I almost didn't make it.' The announcer ignored what Mike said then said, 'Mike, you've been in Wayne's World and created Austin Powers . . .' Mike looked over at me with a knowing glance that said, 'Oh well, funny story out the window.' The radio host didn't even hear it; he had his own agenda. He missed a great story that Mike handed right to him."

In 1998, psychologists Daniel Simmons and Christoper Chabris ran a now famous experiment in which participants were asked to watch a video of people passing basketballs to try to count the number of times one team, those in white shirts, passed the ball. In the middle of the video a person in a gorilla suit walked through the middle of the scene. He stopped, turned, faced the camera, and started pounding on his chest. However, since the research participants were completely focused on the white-shirt team and were trying to ignore the black-shirt team, 51 percent of them missed the gorilla.

The lesson from the gorilla experiment: Realize that your brain is wired to notice what you expect to happen. It's easy to miss the unexpected. If you have predicted what you think is going to happen in a persuasive conversation, you may be so focused on what you expect that you may miss something unexpected from your customer. The "gorilla" you may miss could be a new opportunity your customer hints at, or a new piece of information that can help you build your business relationship with him.

Part of *ditching the pitch* is ditching your preconceived expectations about what could happen. *Be alert* for the unexpected; it might be a gorilla carrying a lot of money.

My guess is that if Simmons and Chabris showed the video to stage improvisers, virtually all of them would spot the gorilla. Improvisational actors are trained to expect the unexpected and never to go into a scene with fixed, preconceived notions.

It's that easy to miss the cues a customer can offer you. If you're not paying close attention to what is happening between you and your customer, you could fail to spot a great opportunity to move the conversation forward. We don't need to worry about knowing what to say next. The hints are right there in front of us. Noticing those hints requires you to be completely present in the current moment.

Be present

It's no secret that staying engaged in the present moment is a challenge for most of us. Too long to-do lists, too many emails, too many text messages, too many interruptions, too many distractions; all of these compete for our attention at every moment, taking us out of the here and now into different places and times. One moment we're paying attention, the next moment we realize that we've been thinking about something that happened yesterday or might happen tomorrow. Our minds jump about, sometimes before we even notice they've left the ground.

Being present is a skill that can be learned with practice. Yvonne Nienstadt, a teacher of meditation at the Rancho La Puerta fitness resort in Tecate, Mexico, remembers, "In the East they call the distracted mind the 'Monkey Mind.' When I took my first steps into trying meditation I found that I had a barrel of monkeys in my head, all making noise and making it hard to meditate. The good news is that with patient, persistent practice I have been able to quiet them all. And if I can, anybody can."

Yvonne continues, "I am not alone in having to confront the chatterbox. Modern science shows that we think between 30,000-60,000 thoughts per day—that's two to three thoughts for every breath we take! Unfortunately, a lot of those thoughts are non-productive, or worse, downright negative. The chatter crowds out our power, our creativity, our inspiration. Our ability to concentrate grows exponentially if we practice being present, every day. We become better listeners and are more responsive to everything and everybody around us."[15]

As Yvonne teaches us, being present is a habit that can be learned. You can practice being present no matter what you are doing, at any time in the day, especially when you are with a customer.

Being present is about paying attention to what is happening around you, without being distracted. But paying attention isn't always easy, as most of us learned by first grade. Here's an idea to help you think about paying attention in a new way.

Put your heart into the situation

The English phrase "pay attention" suggests that attention is a finite resource, and that our allocation of attention is a zero-sum proposition; if you pay attention to one thing, you inherently have less attention to pay to something else. Since we have become so busy, and have so many things to think about, we are frugal with our attention, paying only enough attention to a situation as is minimally required in order to keep other precious bits of attention in reserve for other needs.

Contrast that with the Hebrew idiom for paying attention, *sim lev*, which translates literally as "put heart." If I tell a friend in Hebrew that I paid attention to something, I literally tell him I "put my heart" into that thing. If *paying* attention is a zero-sum game involving finite resources, "putting my heart" into something is not. I don't need to be frugal with my heart; it is limitless. If you throw yourself fully into a situation with a customer, putting your heart into it, there is no opportunity cost. You have plenty of heart.

Just as a sailor riding the waves is constantly attuned to the subtlest changes in the wind, you are able to detect the slightest nuances of conversation if you put your heart into it. You and your conversation partner can ride the conversation together, creating it in the moment.

RECAP: Be Alert

In a persuasive conversation, be alert so that you can continuously ensure that your words and actions follow and are informed by what you observe and perceive. Be here now! Reduce and remove all other distractions when you are in a persuasive conversation.

*   *   *

PRACTICE: Say Less to Notice More

"The quieter you become, the more you can hear."
—Ram Dass

In the early '90s, I was vice-president of resort marketing for Hyatt Hotels & Resorts. When you work in a job like this, there are a lot of people who want to sell you things. People are constantly trying to get appointments with you, because they have discovered the secrets to filling hotel rooms, attracting big-spender golfers or becoming THE place for destination weddings. I was on many people's list of promising leads. I still remember many details of a particular meeting, even though it happened about twenty years ago. By most measures, this meeting was unimportant and should not have earned a place in my long-term memory, but its remarkable one-sidedness made a lasting impression.

I agreed to this meeting because the person who requested it had an intriguing marketing idea and came highly recommended by a colleague. I greeted him in the lobby, and as we walked back to my office he began talking, telling me about his idea and how he had developed it. He was passionate about his idea and was clearly very excited to be talking about it. As we sat down in my office, he kept talking and, without missing a beat, opened his briefcase to pull out a bound presentation book that described his company, his product, and his novel idea. He started walking me through his presentation when it dawned on me that I hadn't spoken one word since we first said hello in the lobby.

Normally, this kind of situation would make me antsy and impatient, but this time I decided to see how long he would keep talking. As he continued, I noted that his idea was very interesting, but it was clear that he didn't understand my business or the issues that I faced. He was telling me how he could help Hyatt Resorts, but he didn't know what Hyatt Resorts needed from him. He could have easily adapted his recommendations to our needs, but since he wasn't asking me any questions, he had no way to learn anything about our business.

After about twenty-five minutes of non-stop talking, he finished, asking, "So, what do you think?"

"Well, I'll have to think about it. Why don't you leave your materials, and I'll show them to my team and we'll get back to you."

He looked disappointed. "Did I miss anything important?"

"I'm not sure," I answered. "Let me think about it."

Here's what I could have said (but didn't): "The only thing you missed is the target. If you walk into a dark room and throw a dart without turning on the lights, it's a one-in-a-million chance you'll hit a bulls-eye. That is essentially what you did in this meeting."

With only a little bit of information from me, he could have adjusted his story and made it more relevant for Hyatt Resorts. But he wasn't interested in getting information from me, only in giving information to me. He missed the target and he missed the chance to connect with my business and with me. My reaction was "I'll have to think about it" and "We'll get back to you," because his monologue didn't help me see how he could help me. Essentially, he made me do the work of connecting his offering to my business needs.

If he had said less, not only would he have learned more about how to sell to me, I would also have enjoyed the conversation more. In their book *Be Quiet, Be Heard,* Peter and Susan Glaser write that people who speak more than 51 percent of the time during a conversation tend to be more satisfied with the conversation.[16] You can notice this principle in your personal life: Watch people on the receiving end of a monologue. How many of them are enjoying themselves?

Every moment you are talking during a persuasive conversation is a moment you are not listening to your customer. You are listening to yourself. Instead, say less, use your own words sparingly, returning to "input mode" as quickly as possible. Give yourself the chance to be alert and notice cues that can drive your reactions.

> *Every moment you are talking during a persuasive conversation is a moment you are not listening to your customer. You are listening to yourself.*

It's surprising how infrequently stage improvisers interrupt each other. You can watch an improv performance at iO that includes ten or more actors, waiting for one to interrupt the other, and it just doesn't happen. One reason for this, which we will discuss later, is the way accomplished improvisers give and take the focus of a scene between themselves. But the primary reason these actors are able to create a scene without interrupting each other is that they are much more focused on listening and observing than on talking. As Charna Halpern describes it, "We are intent on listening for the whole idea. And we listen between the lines. That's why we don't cut each other off." Improv actors' mouths wait for their ears and eyes, and this extra focus on input creates enough open space for people to say things without getting in each other's way.

Contrast this with business meetings where people are more interested in getting their points across than they are in listening to others. People are constantly starting sentences in the middle of other people's sentences, and people are not alert to cues from colleagues that could improve communication.

If you say less, not only will you notice more, but as Peter and Susan Glaser teach us, your customer will be more likely to enjoy the conversation.

Customers, like all people, are really interesting. So are their stories, and the most interesting parts are often in the details. Conversations are also really interesting, especially if you pay attention to their nuances. If you are alert to the details happening around you, you will notice interesting things that will make it easier to stay engaged in the "now." Even a conversation that, on the surface, seems boring has interesting points if you listen for its details.

Be "mega-curious," focusing your interest on everything your customer says and does. As we will see in our next habit, *Size up the scene*, this curiosity will provide you valuable information for improvising your persuasive conversation. But even before you gather any useful information, your curiosity and interest in the details of the situation you are in will help you be alert and "in the now."

Customers don't always tell you exactly what they are thinking. Sometimes they don't want to share everything; sometimes they aren't even aware of everything they are thinking and feeling. It's up to you to listen for and notice the unspoken meaning. When you say less in a conversation, you will be more alert and will be able to detect hidden layers of meaning that lie beneath the words. You may notice a customer's hesitation as he tells you about something, which might indicate that he in especially concerned about a certain issue. He may subtly allude to a problem he is having. He might start talking a bit faster, telling you he is particularly interested in the current subject of the conversation.

But you won't notice all these hidden cues if you are more focused on telling your customer about you than you are on listening to him. Say less to notice more and you will be able to develop more effective and enjoyable persuasive conversations.

* 　 * 　 *

🌀 PRACTICE: Turn Down Your Analytic Brain

Imagine if two kids were going to play cowboys and Indians, and they decided to script it before they started playing, because they were afraid of how they were being observed and afraid they were not going to be effective in the way they played. How much humanity, how much spontaneity, how much fun goes away. Then, imagine that after they did it they decided to sit around for an hour and evaluate their effectiveness in playing cowboys and Indians. That's what adults do, all the time.

—MICK NAPIER

The key is not to be judging yourself, your partner or the thing that's happening.

—ANNE LIBERA

When I spoke with Anne Libera, Director of Comedy Studies at Second City and author of *The Second City Almanac of Improvisation,* I asked her to describe some of the characteristics that make certain people good at improvisation. Without hesitation she said that good improvisers "turn down their analytic brains." She continued, "It's not that we completely turn off our analytic brain, but we turn down the part of our brain that says, 'No, that's not good enough.' When people turn down their analytic brains, they're able to take their focus off of themselves, for the most part, getting out of their own head into the situation that's around them." In other words, if you overanalyze, you won't notice or be able to collect input from your surroundings.

I'm sure we can all relate to what Anne is saying. It's very easy to over-analyze what we are doing, letting self-judgment get in the way of our creativity. Anne recognizes that we can't totally turn off our analytic brains, but if we can keep them down to a "low hum" we will be able to limit self-judgment and self-criticism and free ourselves up to improvise brilliant ideas.

Anne's ideas have been formed by her years in the theater, and there are some recent scientific findings that support what she is saying.

Charles Limb is a professor of Otolaryngology (ear, nose, and throat) at the Johns Hopkins School of Medicine, and is also on the faculty of the Peabody Conservatory of Music. Dr. Limb is fascinated by music, sound and the way the brain interprets what we hear, and he has combined all of his interests in his research. In a recent TEDx MidAtlantic talk called "Your Brain On Improv,"[17] Limb shared results of research where he put jazz musicians in an fMRI (functional magnetic resonance imaging) scanner and monitored their brains while they were improvising.

Limb outfitted an electronic keyboard to work in the fMRI scanner. He asked jazz players to play two kinds of musical pieces while in the fMRI machine—a written piece that they would learn ahead of time and an improvisation over the same musical chords that were in the written piece. His goal was to compare the subjects' brain activity when playing a pre-learned piece with the activity that occurs when improvising.

What Limb found was that, during improvisation, the medial pre-frontal cortex, which is associated with self-expression, had expanded activity, and the lateral pre-frontal cortex, which is associated with self-monitoring, had decreased activity. Limb's findings confirmed what Anne Libera had witnessed in her countless hours teaching improvisation and directing shows at Second City in Chicago: improvisation requires us to turn down our analytic self-judgment, and just let ourselves go. The best improvisers are able to do this, and if you spend too much energy analyzing and judging yourself, you will not be able to generate creative ideas spontaneously.

Imagine if you are with a customer, engaged in a persuasive conversation, and you suddenly say something that you immediately regret. You regret it so much that you can't stop thinking about it, and you begin worrying that your customer will think you are a fool, or at least not the person he thought you were. Your self-flagellation continues to escalate, as you feel beads of sweat accumulate under your shirt collar. Is this productive?

I'm not recommending that you ignore your mistake. It's ok to notice that you've said the wrong thing, for two reasons: you want to recover and take the conversation in a better direction, and you want to learn from the experience so you won't make this mistake again. But it is critical that you assess without judging yourself, because once you judge yourself, you are likely to become distracted and inattentive. If you are criticizing yourself, you may miss something important your customer says.

Similarly, it is important to assess your customer without judgment. He may say something that isn't as brilliant as you might have expected, or he might say something you just don't agree with. Notice it. Assess the situation. But don't judge. Focus instead on understanding what has happened so you can be alert to its implications. Ask yourself, "What can I learn from this? What does this new information mean to the unfolding sales process?"

Or what if you and a colleague are working together, persuading a third person, and he says or does something you don't like? Again, assess without judgment. Your colleague's misstep should not distract you from creating a great persuasive conversation with your customer. We'll focus more on improvisational techniques to implement when selling with colleagues in a later section called "The Persuasion Ensemble."

Whether it is you, your customer, or a colleague, assess without judgment, or you may end up as the one being judged.

Similarly, being self-conscious can distract your thinking. A prom-date scene I saw once at Second City: An actor playing a "guy" (Brendan Jennings) picks a girl from the audience to be his date. He pulls her up on stage, asks her name and some other questions about her. Then the actors begin to create a scene, incorporating the facts they learn about her, which include picking her up at her parents' house, awkwardly pinning a corsage on her dress, slow-dancing, getting crowned prom king and queen, etc. The audience member, Kim, was a great sport, participating in everything the actors threw her way. But if you had walked in during the middle of the scene, and been asked to identify the audience member on stage, you would have been able to do it immediately. Kim had an embarrassed expression on her face, her shoulders were hunched up, and she walked stiffly. She was completely self-conscious, much more focused on what she looked like and what her friends would say later than she was focused on being in the scene.

In all fairness, Kim is not an actress, and the situation caught her by surprise. She deserved all the applause she got from the audience and actors after the scene. But the same thing can happen to a salesperson, and it's less likely he'll get away with it.

Self-consciousness can grab you out of being engaged in the moment with your customer, and deposit you right inside your own head. A good persuader learns to be comfortable in her own skin, putting self-doubt and self-criticism aside.

Robert Cialdini, in his wonderful book *Influence,* writes that communicating confidence is one of the best ways to persuade another person; we are much more likely to believe a person who appears confident.[18] But, looking confident is not enough. It is equally important to be confident that you have the skills to *ditch the pitch.* Once you start over-evaluating and criticizing yourself, you will take yourself out of the moment and lose touch with the details of what's going on between you and your customer.

Being distracted by outcomes is another way in which you can lose touch. Salespeople are taught from their first days of sales training to "go for the close." This is great advice, and, of course, any worthy process of persuasion must ultimately create positive outcomes. But an over-focus on "the close" can create major distractions in a persuasive conversation.

One of my favorite stories to illustrate this point involves two men watching a tightrope walker making a crossing with no net below him. One of the men watching from below says to his friend, "I wonder how he does that." His friend says, "I don't know, but I'm sure he's not thinking about how much he's getting paid." If a salesperson is too focused on the outcome of a conversation, his mind won't be in the moment. He'll either be thinking about what to do with the commission he'll make on this sale, or he'll be preoccupied about what will happen if he doesn't make the sale. Similarly, someone in a non-sales role will diminish his chances of successful persuasion if he is overly concerned with and distracted by the outcomes he is trying to achieve.

Stage improvisers know that one of the surest ways to ruin a scene is to think too soon about how the scene will end. Once they start focusing on the final line and the ensuing applause, their minds won't be engaged in the current moment and they'll miss what is happening right now. Also, aiming for a particular scene climax might lead them to miss an opportunity for a different, possibly better, ending for the scene.

Similarly, if a person is too focused on what he will get from the persuasive conversation, especially if he is too anxious about closing a sale, he will most likely be too distracted by these outcomes to be fully engaged in the conversation. If he is not engaged in the present moment, he may not notice important information and subtle cues from his customer, and miss opportunities to take the conversation to a better place. Ironically, being too focused on the outcome will reduce his chances of realizing that outcome.

RECAP: Turn Down Your Analytic Brain

Remember that over-thinking destroys spontaneity. Don't think too much, don't judge yourself, don't judge others. Keep the analysis in the background and keep the fresh observations and perceptions top of mind.

*   *   *

HABIT #2
Size Up The Scene

SCENE: You meet a long-time customer for lunch and, to your surprise, he has brought someone else from his office. He introduces this person as his new boss. "Hmmm," you think to yourself, "I didn't know he had a new boss." As you sit down and start your conversation, you notice the new boss passing notes to your customer, who stops talking to you each time he receives a note in order to say something back to his boss. The new boss seems unsettled and fidgets constantly as you and your customer talk. It's difficult for you to discern how your customer feels about the situation. You quickly realize that you need to understand this new boss's character and how his involvement will affect your relationship with this company. Figuring this out is suddenly a major goal for you in this conversation.

As actors start an improvised scene, they don't know what is going on in that scene, because the scene hasn't yet been written. As they start improvising they are paying close attention as the scene develops so they can *Size up the scene.*

What does it mean to *Size up the scene?* It is simply to answer the questions: *"What's going on here?" "Who is in the room with me?"* and *"What situation are we in?"*

When improv actors begin a scene, it is implied that the characters were already doing something before the scene started; I've never seen an improv scene that started with the Big Bang. Similarly, every situation you walk into with a customer already has something going on in it before you arrive. You are walking into a moment in progress. One of the first things you must do, as you enter your customer's situation, is be a witness to what is going on as you arrive.

As improv actors *Size up a scene* as that scene begins, there are two areas they are trying to figure out:

(1) Character—who are the people in this scene? What are their motivations and personal characteristics? What are the relationships between the characters? What character does each actor want to portray?

(2) Context—what's happening? What is the situation that the characters find themselves in?

Notice that plot is not one of the first two things that the improv actor is trying to figure out. Forcing plot into the scene too quickly won't work because that plot may not fit the characters and context. Plot will follow naturally as the characters and context become clear.

To *ditch the pitch* in a persuasive conversation, you also need to start by figuring out the characters and the context. When I interviewed Alex von Bidder, co-owner of the legendary Four Seasons Restaurant in New York, he described how his servers *Size up the scene.* "It's about reading the table. And you can get non-verbal cues faster than you can get verbal cues. You can tell if this is a business meeting or an intimate personal time, or you might see that it is a couple who doesn't talk to each other anymore, who might want you to be in-between them."[19]

Similar to how improv actors try to understand character and context, when *ditching the pitch* you need to be clear about:

- *Who* you are dealing with and what you want your customer to think about *who* you are, and

- The situation you and your customer find yourselves in.

Let's explore both of those issues.

❄ PRACTICE: Know Who You Are With

Character—your customer's

> *Learn to discover human nature instead of what you want the scene to be about.*[20]
> —The Second City Almanac of Improvisation

> *Scenes are not about your plot or about your funny. They are about people.*[21]
> —Susan Messing

Improv scenes often start with suggestions from the audience. I remember one scene at The Second City in which the actors received the suggestion "airplane pilots." One actor, Brendan Jennings, immediately assumed the right-hand co-pilot's seat in a cockpit, while another actor sat to his left as captain, and a third sat behind them as the navigator. Brendan, as co-pilot, immediately started portraying a happy-go-lucky, immature personality, with a foolish grin on his face as he started fiddling playfully with imaginary knobs and dials in front of him. The other two actors immediately picked up on the co-pilot's personality, and assumed more serious personalities as they began to interact with their childish colleague. So they were creating a scene that revolved around a co-pilot who had no business being in a 747 cockpit. The other actors' alertness to the co-pilot's personality was the key ingredient that launched the scene.

I find that this example translates perfectly as a lesson for persuasive conversations (except nobody needs to act foolish!) Sales pitches focus on presentation. Persuasive conversations focus on people. Understanding the characters in a persuasive conversation is a critical first step to *ditching the pitch* effectively.

●●●●●●●●●●●●●●●●●●●●

Sales pitches focus on presentation. Persuasive conversations focus on people.

●●●●●●●●●●●●●●●●●●●●

Getting a sense of your customer's personality, motivations, and characteristics can provide you with some of the most valuable input you can find for improvising a persuasive conversation. What is her communication style? What does she seem to care about? Who is she?

I had the opportunity to spend four hours with a prospective client recently. He had asked me to fly to his city to meet with him to discuss a consulting project. We talked in a coffee shop for an hour and a half, after which we embarked on a twenty-five-minute walk through the downtown section of his beautiful city on a summer day, ending up at a restaurant for a long lunch. Although we had spoken by phone previously, this was our first in-person meeting.

As we talked, I was able learn a lot about my new client, all of which helped me understand him better. I observed his communication style, saw clues into his personality, heard about his personal history, and noticed what issues seemed to catch his attention the most. As I began to understand him better as a person, I also began to understand the best ways to interest him in working with me as a consultant. His character gave me many cues about how to proceed.

For example, I noticed that he had a sharp mind and liked to brainstorm ideas. Also, he seemed willing to take risks to improve his business and was willing to make a bold recommendation to the owner of his company to fund the project we were discussing. These things told me a lot about how to interact with him; to interest him I should challenge him with ideas and talk about how we could communicate his vision to his boss. I should focus more on "what could be" instead of "here are the problems you might encounter." Conversely, if I had seen early in the conversation that he was unsure of himself and worried that his job was at risk if the project failed, I would have navigated the conversation differently.

Most marketing and sales training teaches people to group customers together into "segments" based on characteristics that are shared by all customers in the segment. We aren't taught to look for the things that make individual customers unique, because in the mass marketing mindset that has ruled sales and marketing for the better part of a century, this isn't cost-effective. So instead, mass-marketers profile customers and lump them into groups with other customers who are supposedly like them in one or more ways. Examples of these kinds of segments are "males 18 to 34 years of age," "residents of zip code 60015," or "all guests who have visited our restaurant for an anniversary dinner."

Customer segmentation makes life easier for salespeople and marketers, but it can lead them to miss the unique details of the one person you are trying to persuade. For example, imagine you are selling cars and a couple comes into the showroom with two toddlers in strollers, and they ask to see minivans and SUVs. If you assume they are just a typical young family who wants a van or SUV for carting their kids around, you may miss that the husband is a sculptor who needs to transport large pieces of metal, and the wife is in a rock band and wants a car that can easily fit her drum set. You might start talking about child safety features and describe how the SUV has plenty of room for groceries, missing the opportunity to talk about how your vehicles can also accommodate sculptures and cymbals. If you focus first on understanding the

> *I urge people to remember that even classifying these customers amounts to having a standard pitch for them, and that's when you get in trouble.*
> —ALEX von BIDDER OF THE FOUR SEASONS RESTAURANT

individual characters with whom you are interacting before beginning *your* story, you will eventually be able to create a *shared* story that is much richer and much more interesting to these customers.

In our interview, Alex von Bidder, the co-owner of the Four Seasons Restaurant in New York, described it this way: "No two customers are alike. So therefore we need to listen carefully to understand each customer. I urge people to remember that even classifying these customers amounts to having a standard pitch for them, and that's when you get in trouble."

Character—yours

> *The first three seconds in a scene is your promise to the audience about who you will be.*[22]
>
> —Susan Messing
> On an important lesson she learned from improv actor Mick Napier

When Brendan Jennings portrayed a foolish 747 co-pilot in the scene previously described, he helped his fellow performers by communicating a very clear character at the top of the scene. The personal characteristics he displayed were gifts to his fellow actors, helping them figure out how they would react to and interact with him.

Matt Hovde, director of The Second City mainstage shows and artistic director of the Second City Training Center, says that the most important thing a stage improviser can do at the beginning of a scene is to establish his character. "Don't go into a scene with expectations," Matt teaches, "go in with a point of view because that's what a character really is." This is important, Matt continues, "because from the moment the scene starts, the audience is desperately trying to answer questions that pop into their heads. They're wondering, 'Who is she?' 'What is she like?' 'What is happening?' Once they answer some of those questions, they relax and enjoy what's happening. Eventually, if actors haven't answered any questions about who they are or what's happening, the audience gives up."[23]

Consider what kinds of questions a customer has about you at the beginning of a persuasive conversation. Whether it is a potential customer you are meeting for the first time, or a person you have known for a long time, this person probably has similar questions about you in his head. He's more likely to be wondering about you than he is to be thinking about your product's features and benefits. So help him answer those questions.

A new customer you meet is more likely to be wondering about you than he is to be thinking about your product's features and benefits.

By giving your customer clear clues about who you are, you are making it easier for him to interact with you. You are giving him bearings that will help him navigate the conversation.

Long before telling your customer about what you are offering him you want your customer to understand who you are. This is true in all kinds of persuasive situations. If you are persuading a large company's general counsel to hire your law firm for a million dollar case, or if you are persuading a young couple to hire you to paint their house, the same holds true. In each case the customer is doing business with you, not with your legal briefs or your paint. Communicate who you are before you try to communicate what you want to sell.

Communicate who you are before you try to communicate what you want to sell.

All masks are empty until they are inhabited by the actor.[24]
—THE SECOND CITY ALMANAC OF IMPROVISATION

Often when I am hired to speak at a conference, the organizers ask me to "send my presentation" to them in advance. Obviously, what they are looking for is a PowerPoint presentation or any printed materials I might be using as handouts.

However, it's impossible to send a presentation ahead of time because the presentation is created as I am on the stage. I often give audiences printed materials to take home, but these printouts are not my presentation.

Just as all masks are empty until inhabited by an actor, all persuasive situations are empty until inhabited by the persuader. A person who focuses his time on preparing a pitch has the tendency to mistake the prepared pitch for the persuasive conversation. But a sales presentation has no life until the salesperson brings it to life. Don't mistake your PowerPoint presentation, your sales collateral, or your product list for your sales effort. They are empty until you bring them to life.

Similarly, if you are trying to persuade a work colleague, a friend or a family member to do something, don't mistake your logic and rationale for the persuasive effort. Nothing happens until you bring your logic to life in a rich, persuasive conversation.

Recap: Know Who You Are With

Focus on "who" before "what." Understand your characters before developing a story.

*   *   *

🌀 PRACTICE: Understand the Context of Your Conversation

Sometimes it's easy to know what's going on when a scene starts, such as in the first minutes of *Saving Private Ryan.* You'd have to be in a coma not to notice that the movie opens in the middle of the D-Day invasion. Other times, however, it's much more difficult to get an immediate idea of what is happening, such as at the beginning of

The Matrix or *The Sixth Sense*, and you have to work a little harder to understand the context. Sometimes it's easy to get an idea of what's going on, and sometimes it isn't so easy.

Just as stage improvisers need to understand quickly who the characters are in a scene, they also need to make quick assessments about the context they are in. Where are we? What is happening? Is it night or day? Are we outside or inside? What's the weather like?

In a persuasive conversation your ability to improvise is increased with each understanding you glean about the context you and your customer find yourselves in. I received a call recently from the president of a company, a former client for whom I had not done consulting work in a while. As we started talking, I was listening for clues about what was going on in his business and why he was calling. I heard that his vice president of marketing had left the company, what challenges he was encountering, and which new products were achieving the best success. As I pieced together a picture of what was going on in the company, I became much more prepared for an effective persuasive conversation.

Here are some examples of things to look for as you try to understand the context of your persuasive conversation with a customer, whether the customer is a sales prospect, a current customer, or a work colleague:

- What's going on in your customer's business or personal life?

- What outside forces are affecting your customer or what kinds of outside forces your customer thinks are affecting him?

- How ready is your customer to make a decision or commitment?

- How easy it is for your customer to make a decision?

- Where your customer's overall focus is these days?

If the customer is a sales prospect, here are some particular things to look for:

- How qualified is this person to be your customer?

- What kinds of purchases does this person already make of products or services similar to yours?

- Who else do they buy from?

●●●●●●●●●●●●●●●●●●●

In the spirit of "input before output," knowledge of the context will fuel what you say and do.

●●●●●●●●●●●●●●●●●●●

As you begin to understand the context surrounding your conversation, you will find that you are improvising more freely. In the spirit of "input before output," knowledge of the context will fuel what you say and do.

Characters are defined by their relationships

Characters don't exist in a vacuum; they are defined by their relationships.[25]

—THE SECOND CITY ALMANAC OF IMPROVISATION

When you watch a theater piece or a movie, your interest is not only drawn to characters but to the relationships between those characters. Shakespeare's Falstaff and Prince Hal are both fascinating characters, but it is the relationship between them that fuels the Henry IV and Henry V plays. In *Casablanca*, Rick and Ilsa are both magnificent characters, but it is their relationship that defines the film.

Understanding relationships is one of the first cues that helps an audience (and the actors!) understand what is going on in an improv scene. I remember an improvised scene at The Second City that began with a male actor standing at stage right. A woman entered from stage left and they said hello. At that point, I had no idea who they were or what their relationship was. And neither did they. Then the woman said, "Sorry to bother you. I just wanted to talk with you, you know, mother-in-law to son-in-law."

With that one line, the possibilities in the scene were narrowed from every possible situation between a man and a woman to situations that could arise between a mother-in-law and her son-in-law. As an audience member, I could discern a frame of reference, and was now invested in seeing what would happen next. As the next few lines were spoken, they were able to define their mother-in-law/son-in-law relationship further, which advanced the scene.

The improvising actors began to develop a situation where the son-in-law came home with his new wife to the small town where she grew up so he could enter the local pie-baking contest. The mother-in-law described how nervous she was about the contest, and how she hoped her son-in-law wouldn't embarrass the family by making a bad pie. The audience quickly understood that it was a summer day, and that the town was small enough to have the tradition of an annual pie-baking contest. As the context became clear, we became grounded and further engaged in the scene.

The main premise of my book *We: The Ideal Customer Relationship* is that relationships are much more captivating for customers than products or services are. I have seen time and again in research related to my consulting practice that customers are more likely to believe a company is unique if they have a "We" relationship with it than if they don't. This is not surprising; we have evolved as social beings, and have been engaging in relationships with members of our own species for millions of years longer than we have been analyzing product specifications and comparison-shopping.

This has many implications for *ditching the pitch*. First, it is important for you to understand your customers' relationship with other involved parties in order to *Size up a scene* and understand the context of what's going on. In the scene I described at the beginning of this section, it was important to understand the relationship between your customer and his new boss. Similarly, if you are a contractor trying to sell a home remodeling job to a couple, you must to understand what the dynamic is between the wife and husband, and the way their relationship is affecting the way they will make decisions about their home improvements. Or, if you are a vice-president of human resources trying to sell your CEO, COO, and CFO on a new project, you must understand the relationships between these three executives if you are to navigate the persuasive process successfully. Just as you can understand Rick and Ilsa's situation in *Casablanca* by understanding their relationship, you can better understand your customers' situation by understanding their relationships, with you and with others.

Second, be clear about the relationship you establish between your customer and yourself. How do you want your customer to think about your relationship? What level of familiarity is optimal? Are you a confidant? Are you a sage advisor? A coach? A peer? An outside expert? An outside partner? A team player? A friend? Do you share humor? What level of personal relationship is appropriate and effective for this situation? Are you able to create a "We" relationship, in which your customer focuses on you as a collaborative partner?

> **What your customer feels about his relationship with you will form the foundation of how he views your product and service offerings.**

What your customer feels about his relationship with you will form the foundation of how he views your product and service offerings. Relationships are very reliable communicators of situations and character features. The shared story you will ultimately build with your customer blossoms out of your relationship. This holds true for long-term customer relationships, such as those relationships architects, lawyers, financial planners, and consultants have with their clients.

This also holds true for short-term relationships, such as a ten-minute relationship a retail salesperson may have with a customer buying a television or a sweater in the course of one visit to a store. Every human interaction affects the relationship between the people involved. The salesperson that dispenses product features in a transactional manner will not build a relationship and is no more effective than an impersonal electronic kiosk. The salesperson who creates a relationship-building encounter, even if it only lasts for a few minutes, will do a much more effective job at communicating the reasons for buying from her.

> ### Recap: Know Your Customer's Situation
>
> Don't ever guess your customer's situation, especially when you make statements that can be affected by that situation. Always seek to understand "what's going on" and always recognize that there is something deeper behind it.

*   *   *

PRACTICE: Listen for the Game

Have you ever been in a conversation and realized that you and the other person are actually having two separate conversations? (Just listen to two people with opposing views discuss politics.)

Improv actors are very conscious of perceiving the "game" going on in a scene. By the game they mean: What are we really doing? What are we really talking about? What's really going on here?

As a scene develops, the actors on stage begin to perceive the game, and they find common ground in which to play. As they establish character and context, they begin to sense what's happening in the scene. As they converge upon the "game" they are able build the scene together.

The same thing happens in a conversation. A conversation is much more likely to flow if the participants in the conversation agree, tacitly, on the "game" of the conversation. When you are in a persuasive conversation, try to spot the emerging game, and adapt your conversation to this game.

Recently I met with a prospective client. Going into the conversation I believed that his biggest needs were clarifying his brand story and continuing his double-digit growth. As we toured his plant and talked, I came to realize that his biggest priorities were fixing his sales process and increasing the share of each customer's business that he received.

I also gleaned insights into his character and which issues were most urgent to him. In other words, I saw that the "game" of the conversation was different than I had originally thought. Because I was listening for the game, it wasn't hard to flex and adapt to what I perceived, and it resulted in a very successful persuasive conversation.

Recap: Listen for the Game

As a persuasive conversation develops, listen for "the game." Be aware of the dynamic this game creates between you and your customer, and adapt your approach to the conversation accordingly.

*　　　*　　　*

The co-pilot described at the beginning of this chapter was giving his fellow actors a very valuable gift when he displayed clear personality characteristics. Stage improvisers are taught to give gifts to their fellow actors in many ways: giving each other names, communicating what their relationship is, describing the context they are in.

Similarly, you can look at everything your customer says or does as a gift that helps you *Figure out what's going on.* Even if he communicates impatience or frustration, he is giving you valuable information that can help you respond in an appropriate way. To *ditch the pitch,* develop the habit of *Thinking input before output,* and you'll notice the cues that will help you develop a persuasive conversation. As the conversation continues, develop the habit of *Sizing up the scene* in order to understand important pieces of your customer's story.

If you follow the advice of Ram Dass: "The next message you need is always right where you are," you will be able to *Figure out what's going on* and persuade others more effectively.

Go with the Flow

HOW TO PROPEL A PERSUASIVE CONVERSATION FORWARD

As you take stock of what is happening in a persuasive conversation, your next move is to propel the conversation forward. You want to create a rich back-and-forth dialogue that builds upon itself and continues to engage both you and your customer deeper into the conversation.

A conversation is a fragile thing. One moment it is cruising along, and the next moment it can stall. One moment it is robust, and the next moment it can be weak. The quality of your persuasive conversation depends on how well you and your customer are moving in sync, like two dancers waltzing in a synchronized flow of mutual affirmation and agreement.

To understand this fluidity, look no further than your everyday conversations. How does a conversation that is based on mutual affirmation and agreement feel compared to one that is either contentious or disconnected?

Let's explore our first habit to help us *Go with the flow:* Create a series of "Yeses."

HABIT #3

Create a Series of "Yeses"

SCENE: I arrive at my client's office a few minutes before 10:00 a.m. in plenty of time for our meeting. I know he's got a tight schedule this morning, and we'll need every minute before his next meeting at 11:00 to review my proposal for a new project. I wait in the lobby until 10:15, when he finally comes out and says, "Steve, sorry I'm late, but I have to run out to the plant to see the shift supervisor. Mind walking with me?"

Of course I'm disappointed, since I know we won't be able to discuss the details of the proposal while we're walking. But, what choice do I have? "Sure Bill. Let's go. I haven't been out to your plant since you installed your new production line."

It's far more interesting to say "yes."—Charna Halpern

A sale is a series of yeses.[26]—Alan Weiss, author

Life often unfolds in unexpected ways. When this happens we can say "no" and resist the new reality, denying and protesting every unanticipated thing that happens, or we can say "yes" and adapt to reality as it changes. The best music and stage improvisers know how to *Go with the flow* and accept everything that happens, as it happens. They know that to deny what happens around them is to kill creativity.

The same thing happens in an effective persuasive conversation. Each time you or your customer says "no" the conversation loses momentum. Your goal, at every moment, is to advance the conversation, and at the same time advance your relationship. Does that mean you need to agree with everything your customer says? No, it doesn't. But even when you need to communicate "no," you can communicate a feeling of "yes" in a way that keeps the conversation moving forward.

Let's explore how . . .

✷ PRACTICE: Say "Yes, and . . ."

Saying "yes" is the most important foundational principle of stage or music improvisation. No matter what your fellow actors or musicians say, do, or play, it is important not to resist it or deny it. You want to accept it and build upon it.

If you listen to a jazz performance, you will notice that the players take turns playing improvised solos over the backing support of their band mates. As each musician plays his improvised solo, the other musicians listen carefully and adjust their playing to what the soloist does. If the soloist increases the intensity of his playing, the band follows. If the soloist brings the intensity down, opting for a mellower, sweeter feel, the band adjusts. If the soloist emphasizes a particular rhythmic pattern, you will often hear the drummer echoing that pattern in his playing. The band says "yes" to whatever the soloist does.

I saw an improvised stage show at Chicago's Annoyance Theater recently with improv actors and Second City veterans Susan Messing and Neil McNamara. In one scene, Neil was playing the role of a grandfather telling stories about his experiences in war, and Susan was playing his bored granddaughter. At one point, Neil said, "And then I got shot and ended up in the hospital." Susan immediately jumped out of her chair, walked behind Neil as she made a noise of beeping hospital machines, and appeared at Neil's opposite side as a nurse, and offered him medications. Neil, who had already been slouching back in his chair, leaned back further as if he were his younger self in a hospital bed, and they exchanged a few lines as nurse and patient. Then Susan dashed back to her chair, resumed the character of the granddaughter, and Neil continued the scene as the elderly grandpa.

This entire portion of Neil and Susan's show took no more than a minute, yet it was filled with many "yeses." Susan said "yes" to Neil's mention of the hospital by assuming the character of Neil's nurse. Neil agreed with Susan's change of time, place, and character, and said "yes" by immediately transporting his character back to war time and pretending to be in a hospital bed. Then, when Susan suggested going back to the present time by once again becoming the granddaughter, Neil again agreed and transitioned back to being the grandfather in the chair. The result was an effective side-scene that was as smooth as if it had been pre-conceived, which of course it wasn't.

Similarly, agreeing with the flow of the conversation, saying "yes" to whatever happens, is the foundation of propelling a persuasive conversation forward. To keep your customer engaged with you, you have to accept every little twist and turn she throws into the conversation, using these twists and turns as opportunities to move the conversation ahead. If you deny what your customer brings into the conversation, you risk shutting the conversation down. You never want to force your customer to go in a direction she does not want to go in. You want to create a flowing persuasive conversation, in which you and your customer are moving together, not in opposition. Alex von Bidder of the Four Seasons Restaurant says, "I try to answer customers' questions with as many yeses as I can."

Let's say you are a salesperson and you sit down with a customer, expecting to sign a contract renewal. In the past few weeks, you have worked hard to iron out all of the details of this contract, and today's meeting was planned as nothing more than an exchange of signatures. However, as you start your meeting, your customer says, "I've been thinking about the clause on page 23 that describes penalties if we cancel orders."

Your immediate reaction is frustration. You and your customer have spent a long time discussing this issue, and you thought you had already reached a reasonable compromise. You may be tempted to blurt out, "What? You're bringing that up now? Why didn't you mention these concerns two weeks ago when we reached an agreement about the cancellation policy?" but that would be totally counterproductive. Instead, you accept what your customer has just said and say, "Let's take a look at it and see if our earlier discussions have addressed both of our concerns."

The first reaction immediately puts your customer on the defensive. As you go into a fighting posture, so does he, and your dialogue grinds to a halt. The second reaction, in which you effectively say "yes," is actually a much more productive means to get your way, because you are collaborating with him to address his concern. You are supporting the conversation, not shutting it down. You are disappointed that he wants to talk about the cancellation policy, but if you can keep him from going into a defensive mode, you will find it much easier to bring him back to the point in the conversation where you compromised two weeks ago.

Additionally, the second reaction where you say "yes," enables you to learn what your customer is really thinking. Maybe he just wants you to help him come up with a way to persuade his boss that the penalty clause is reasonable. Maybe he's just not clear about what the penalties are. By saying "yes" you will learn what his real issues are and be able to keep the conversation moving forward.

Notice that you don't have to use the word "yes" to say "yes." Any agreement to move the conversation forward feels like "yes" to your customer, and makes you feel like his ally.

Does this sound a bit frightening, always saying, "Yes" to your customer? Don't worry, I'm not suggesting that you acquiesce to everything your customer wants, or to reduce your price just because your customer asks you to, or to cave in on unreasonable requests. As we will see, there are ways to say "yes" to every situation, improving your conversation and relationship with your customer without compromising your position.

As students of stage improvisation are taught, saying "yes" doesn't stop when you say "yes." After you say "yes," you build on what the other actors say or do, adding and enriching it with your response. This principle is called "Yes, and . . .," and it is one of the most universal rules of improvisation.

In the example given above, Neil and Susan didn't just say "yes" to each other's words and actions, they *Said "yes, and . . ."* as they built upon the other's ideas. It's as if they said "Yes, I hear what you have said, and I want to offer you something that builds upon it."

Following "yes" with "and" in a persuasive conversation is very important. Imagine you are a housing contractor, trying to persuade a client to put synthetic siding on his house, and the client says, "I think natural wood siding looks much better. I want wood." You can answer, "Yes, wood looks great," but that wouldn't help your sales effort very much! If instead you answered, "***Yes***, wood looks great, ***and*** we have many new options that look as good as wood at a much lower cost." Without the "and" you'd be missing the chance to bring the conversation in the direction you want to take it.

You can spot examples of "Yes, and . . ." anytime you listen to improvised dialogue among comedians. Watch Jon Stewart any time he interviews another comedian on *The Daily Show*. The entire interview is built on a series of "Yes, and . . ." exchanges, as each performer accepts and then builds upon what the other has said.

There is always something to say "yes" to

You're probably already thinking, "Ok, I get the concept, but what about the times I have to say 'no'? I can't always say 'yes' to everything my customers say."

Even when you have to say "no," the concept of "Yes, and . . ." can be used to keep a persuasive conversation moving forward in a collaborative way. Imagine that you work for an advertising agency, and just as you are putting the finishing touches on a new campaign your client calls and says, "I've been having second thoughts about one of the photos in our magazine ads, and I want to change it. But I still want the campaign to launch on the 25th of the month." You know for certain that it will be impossible to change the photo without the launch date slipping, since the deadline is tight and your media department is already bugging you for the finished ads.

But instead of saying, "No, that's impossible," you could say, "**Yes**, we can talk about that. Tell me what you don't like about the photo, **and** we'll look at all our options. As you know, our deadline is tight, and we will have to choose between the launch date and changing the photo. We can make that decision together." "Yes, and . . ." will keep your client from getting defensive, and you will have a much easier time finding a sensible resolution to the problem.

There is always something you can yes to. In this case, you didn't say "yes" to changing the photo, you said "yes" to looking at all of the options. This isn't the least bit disingenuous; after all, after you look at all the options your client may decide the deadline is more important than the photo.

The most obvious example of finding something different to say yes to is the situation where a customer asks you to reduce prices. Recently, I was reviewing a consulting project proposal with a prospective client when he said, "We want to do this project, but the price is too high." I answered with, "**Yes**, this is a substantial investment for your company, **and** I believe it is an investment that will pay you significant returns. It's a very fair price, considering what we are going to do for you and the value you will receive. If you need the price to come down, we can look for ways to reduce the scope of the project. Maybe if we take out a few components of the project we'll be able to get into your budget range."

Notice how I didn't say "yes" to the price being high. I said "yes" to the substantial investment he was going to make. This also wasn't disingenuous; I believed this project was a great investment for him, not just an expense.

By saying "Yes, this is a substantial investment for your company, *and* I believe it is an investment that will pay you significant returns," I was able to avoid the feeling of disagreement and defensiveness that comes with "but." That made it more likely that he would stay engaged enough to hear the next thing I said, that the price could come down if we reduced the scope of the project.

When confronted with a tough situation or a tough comment from a customer, and you feel compelled to say "no," look for something you can say "yes" to. There is always something. Remember our habit: *Think input before output.* You will be able to discover, on the spot, things you can say "yes" to if you are totally alert and completely engaged in the moment with your customer.

RECAP: Say "Yes, and . . ."

A good conversation—and a sale—is a series of yeses. There is always something you can say "yes" to. Find it, follow it with "and," and you will keep your conversation flowing.

*   *   *

🌀 PRACTICE: Work with What You Are Given

Imagine that you come to a meeting with someone who could become your customer and the scene you encounter is not what you expected:

- You meet a prospective customer for lunch and he spends the first 45 minutes telling you about his recent fishing trip.

Or...

- Ten minutes into a meeting with a prospective customer, you realize that her most important business issues aren't anything close to what you thought they'd be.

Or...

- You show up for the big meeting with two key senior executives in your company, hoping to persuade them to let you proceed with a new proposed project. You know you will need the approval of both these executives, but only one of the two shows up for the meeting.

What do you do? Resist? Get upset? Try to deny the situation?

The only thing you can do: Say "yes" to the new situation and *Work with what you are given.*

As we've seen in the examples, stage improvisers become very proficient at working with what they are given. Regardless of what another character says on stage, they build upon it. Or, if an actor is holding a prop and it suddenly breaks, she makes this part of the scene.

Maybe the audience surprises her by laughing at an unexpected moment, but instead of continuing in the direction she had started, she accepts the audience response as a gift and charts a new course in the dialogue.

I remember a scene at the Annoyance Theater by the improv group Fishnuts, when some feathers started to fall from the ceiling at one end of the stage, as if a feather pillow in the sky had suddenly burst open. The actors noticed these ephemeral floaters, went to that side of the stage, and began to integrate a story of a chicken hanging from the ceiling into their scene.

The authors of *The Second City Almanac of Improvisation* encourage improvisers to "ride the events of a scene the way a surfer rides a wave."[27] This is exactly what you must do to create a fluid persuasive conversation. No matter what unexpected surprises arise in a sales meeting, the success of your conversation requires you to *Work with what you are given.* A surfer can control his direction, but only if he uses the current to his advantage. Fight the waves and you fall.

I encountered this challenge recently. Previously, a client had asked me for a proposal for a new project, which I had submitted to them a few weeks ago. Last week, they called to tell me they had looked over the proposal in detail and wanted to review it with me. A few minutes into the phone call, I realized that they hadn't read the proposal carefully, and they had missed some of its most important details. Because of this, they had missed the essence of my recommendations and weren't that excited about the project. They said they wanted to put it off for a few months.

What could I do? Get mad at them for not reading the proposal more carefully? Argue with them and tell them that the best thing for them to do is start the project now? *Scold them?*

Of course not. Their misunderstanding of the proposal became the new reality. I had to work with what I was given.

After recognizing the new context, I had to shift gears and say "yes" to the situation, then determine the best way to use this conversation to communicate the missed details of the proposal.

Was I disappointed? Yes. Did I wish for another reality? Yes. Would I have received approval for the project if I had denied this reality and fought them? No.

Work with what you are given. Use the situation you find yourself in as the starting point for moving the conversation forward. As Anne Libera says, "The place of creativity is in letting every situation be ripe with possibilities."

Earlier, when discussing the importance of alertness, I shared the story of the "invisible gorilla" experiment, where participants in a study didn't notice a person in a gorilla suit walking right through a scene on a video, simply because they weren't expecting it. It's very easy to close yourself off to new information when you are not ready for it to appear.

The result? You miss the chance to say yes without even realizing it.

Earlier, I quoted Chicago improv actor Jessica Rogers, saying: "You must be open to all new pieces of information." This is, essentially, saying "yes" to everything that happens. You don't want to deny anything that happens.

In a persuasive conversation, be fully open to new information and be willing to see that every situation is bursting with limitless possibilities. You may discover a way to work with your customer that you hadn't considered prior to the conversation. As Anne Libera teaches, "You have to trust that when you follow possibilities, something's going to be there. Change will occur, and you will be there at the other side of it."

If you enter a conversation with a customer committed to using a rigid pitch, you most likely will be disappointed because situations rarely turn out exactly as we expect. If, instead, you embrace the surprises that every situation presents, you will see each twist and turn in a persuasive conversation as an opportunity full of new possibilities to advance your relationship with this customer.

Tom Yorton of Second City Communications says, "While each actor's in-the-moment response may not be the best idea, it is always at least a bridge to the best idea."[28] It is impossible for everything you say in a persuasive conversation to be the best thing you could possibly say. Similarly, everything your customer says in a persuasive conversation cannot be the best thing you hope to hear. However, as Tom's quote teaches us, every idea can be a bridge to the best idea. You can always get there from here.

As part of the research for this book, I studied stage improvisation at The Second City in Chicago to learn improv techniques from some of the best actors in the field. Here's an example that I witnessed in one of my classes that illustrates the principle described above: Two of my classmates, Mary and Elise, were improvising a scene, playing two women who were stranded on a lifeboat in the middle of the Atlantic Ocean. In the first few lines they revealed their fear that they might not be rescued. Then, Mary said to Elise, "If we don't make it out of here, it'll be sad that you'll never make it to Europe to start your job as an international goose hunter."

Mary's line came out of nowhere. On first reflection, you might think that this crazy idea of establishing Elise as a would-be international goose hunter could confuse the scene. But that's not what happened. Mary and Elise ran with the idea, and pretty soon they were talking about how their shipwreck might be the primary cause of worldwide geese over-population. The rest of the class was cracking up. Her idea became a bridge to even better ideas.

This principle that every idea is a bridge to the best idea can be very liberating in a persuasive conversation. You'll stress yourself out if you worry that everything you or your customer says must be the perfect thing to say. But if you say, "Yes, and . . ." to everything that happens, focusing on the flow of the conversation and how every moment in the conversation is a bridge to a better place, you can free yourself up and work towards that better place. You can always get there from here.

Let's say that during a persuasive conversation your customer says something that you are disappointed to hear or he shows a lack of interest in the substance of the conversation. Or he says something that shows he has misunderstood some of the things you've said. These responses, while not the responses you would most prefer, give you insights into the best path to get where you want to be. (Remember our habit: *Size up the scene.* You are always looking for information that can help you understand what's going on.) Now you are in a better position to say something that will engage him and get you both closer to the best idea.

This happens to me often when I'm speaking with a prospective client about brand strategy. The prospective customer will speak about his brand as his logo or tagline, which is a much more limited view of branding than I want him to have. I can't say, "That's a pretty limited view of branding." Instead, I look at his comment not as an obstacle but as a starting point that will help me find a bridge to where I want the conversation to be. I now know the course I must navigate, because I know where my customer is starting.

Or what if you say something that is not up to your normal level of pith and insight? Should you panic? Should you end the meeting, go home, and stick your head under a pillow? No! Look at your unfortunate comment as a bridge to the next place you want to be. It may not be the best bridge you want to be on, but since you're already on this bridge, with no way to turn back, you might as well accept the fact that you have to cross it.

Don't get hung up on saying the "right" thing at points in a persuasive conversation. There is no right or wrong, only possibilities and choices. Sure, you may not say the best thing, but it was only a choice you made, and it is a choice from which you can recover. Since every idea is a bridge to the best idea, you can now make another choice, a choice that will lead you to a better place.

> *There is no right or wrong, only possibilities and choices.*

Don't get anxious if you say the "wrong" thing. Instead, *Work with what you are given*, looking for a way to use this "wrong" thing to advance your conversation with a customer. Soon you will surprise yourself when you make a wonderful comment you hadn't expected. Everything you say, or what your customer says, is a bridge to the best idea. *Say, "Yes, and . . ."* and then keep moving across this bridge.

RECAP: Work with What You Are Given

Whatever happens, believe "we can get there from here." Work with what happens, and don't resist the situation, even if it is not optimal.

---

*   *   *

🌀 PRACTICE: Ensure Your Customer Keeps Saying Yes

We have focused mostly on how you can say "yes" to keep a conversation flowing. But it is equally important that your customer is also saying "yes" to you. If your customer says "no" to something you say or disagrees with a statement you make, you will immediately feel the conversation stall.

I remember once when I was meeting with a prospective customer and our conversation was moving along very well. As I listened to this person talk I began to get a good idea of his business situation, or at least I thought I did. At one point I said, "So it seems that the most important issue you are facing is that the decision-makers who buy your product at your customers' companies soon move on to different jobs, and the new person in the job has no idea why his company does business with you." The person stopped, looked at me quizzically, and said, "No, I don't think that's really a very big problem." This was followed by an awkward silence, and I could see the momentum of the conversation disappear like the air from a punctured bicycle tire.

The mistake I made: I gave my customer a chance to say "no."

It is important at all times in a persuasive conversation to focus on creating mutual affirmation and agreement. As noted earlier, "the quality of your persuasive conversation depends on how well you and your customer are moving in sync, like two dancers waltzing in a synchronized flow of mutual affirmation and agreement."

We can understand this issue well by looking at our personal lives. If you are trying to persuade a spouse, significant other, child or parent, think how much more effective your persuasion will be if you can navigate the conversation in a way that avoids compelling the other person to say "no."

Here are a few tips to help you avoid hearing "no" from your customer during a persuasive conversation:

- Don't assume anything. Be careful before making a statement that you are confident it won't put your customer into a defensive mode. If you're not sure, ask. Don't tell.

- Don't prescribe a solution too early. Your primary job in a persuasive conversation is not to advise the customer. It is to move your relationship forward. Only prescribe solutions when your client is ready to hear them. A good persuasive conversation is diagnostic.

- Keep the conversation focused on your customer, not on what you are trying to sell your customer. This is a key principle in

Step 3: This is a key principle in Chapter 6: *Let a shared story emerge through your conversation* on page 97.

- Avoid yes-or-no questions. Phrase your questions, when possible, as a "choice between yeses", i.e., "Which of these two options seems better to you?"

RECAP: Ensure Your Customer Keeps Saying "Yes."

Try to steer clear of the opportunities for your customer to use the word "no." Don't assume and don't prescribe too early.

*   *   *

HABIT #4
Explore and Heighten

SCENE: Gary has a home remodeling business, which has been tough lately so he has taken on some simple handyman jobs until the market turns around. This morning he visited Joe and Kathy Sullivan's home, responding to their call to change the arrangement of shelves in their kitchen pantry. As they explained what they needed, Joe said, "This pantry is designed so poorly that it's difficult to arrange everything in a logical way. We're wasting tons of space."

Kathy added, "Joe likes to have everything close at hand while he cooks, and he gets really frustrated when he can't find things."

"Tell me what you mean." Gary said to Joe. Joe showed Gary the crowded shelves on the right side of the pantry and the empty wall with no shelves adjacent to it. "Isn't this crazy?" Joe asked. "It's hard to find things because everything is so crowded, but we have all this extra unused space."

"Can you show me how you use the pantry so I can come up with some ideas?"

Joe reached into the pantry, hunted around in the back of the shelves and took out a few things, which he then put on the counter. "We don't have a lot of space on the counter, so I have to do my preparation in little stages. It's really a hassle. This whole kitchen was designed poorly."

"How would you like it to work?" Gary asked.

Joe started describing how he'd like to be able to have more room in the pantry. "And, it sure would be nice if I could easily access things I need while I'm cooking. By the time I walk across the kitchen and then find things in the pantry I could burn something, it takes so long."

From there Joe started describing how he'd like to be able to stage his items near the stove, moving around the kitchen, waving his arms as he demonstrated how he'd like things to work. Kathy jumped in to the conversation, saying "I'd love it if we didn't have to cram all the pots and pans into these two small drawers."

Gary asked a few more questions, exploring the Sullivan's frustrations with their kitchen, finding out more about their situation. He responded to what he learned by offering a few ideas of how they could make better use of the space in their kitchen. As the conversation progressed it became clear to all three of them that they weren't only talking about fixing a few shelves in the pantry. They were discussing an entire remodel of the Sullivan's kitchen.

The real "meat" of improvisation is the idea of Explore and Heighten.

—Anne Libera

As we've noted, *Saying, "Yes, and..."* isn't only about being agreeable. It's about moving a conversation forward, and making sure that every idea is a bridge to better ideas.

Stage improvisers employ an idea called *Explore and Heighten* along with the concept of "Yes, and..." described earlier as a springboard to elevate an idea in a scene. As *The Second City Almanac of Improvisation* says, "[When] raising the stakes of the activity . . . if something is fully explored and heightened, a change will happen organically—a transformation will occur."[29]

The idea works like this: When you say "yes" to something that happens in a scene, use the "and" to raise the stakes and take the idea to the next level. Earlier I showed how Susan Messing and Neil McNamara *Explored and heightened* a scene when Susan responded to Neil's comment about getting shot in the war. She explored this idea by taking the scene back in time to the hospital, and then she and Neil were able to heighten the idea through their dialogue.

There are many ways to *Explore and heighten* during a persuasive conversation. Let's say you are selling furniture, and a customer shopping for a couch tells you she has seven cats. You start to explore this piece of information, and you discover that she doesn't believe that cats should be declawed. You are now able to zero in on your toughest, tear-resistant, and stain-resistant fabrics to heighten the conversation by focusing on what is most important to her.

A client of mine at a non-profit organization recently said that he felt his organization could actually make the world a better place to live in. I said, "yes" to his comment and explored the idea with him. In a few minutes of back-and-forth brainstorming and exploration, we had actually identified a persuasive story about how his organization can make the world a better place. I'll admit, his comment seemed a bit ambitious to me at first, but by *Exploring and heightening* the dialogue, as opposed to dismissing his comment, we were able to develop his idea in a very compelling way. This thread of conversation engaged him deeply in our conversation, and served as a key turning point in his decision to hire our firm to do work for him.

Note that in each preceding example the heightening came after the exploration. It is not always apparent how best to heighten an idea until it is explored. There are many times in persuasive conversations where patience is important and this is one of them; don't be anxious about finding breakthroughs, but instead, have the patience to explore an idea, and then see what comes out of it. Very few ideas spill out of people fully formed the first time they say them. Creativity and idea generation are iterative processes where we improve an idea each time we play with it. A collaborative persuasive conversation works the same way, and if you are willing to explore ideas with your customer, you will inevitably heighten those ideas, as long as you both are saying "yes" to what happens in the conversation.

🖜 PRACTICE: Find Your Customer's Path

Sales pitches are designed to have a logical chronology, starting at the beginning and proceeding on from there. On the contrary, persuasive conversations and improv scenes often start in the middle.

Most of the conversations you have in your personal life start in the middle. You run into a friend on the street and you start talking and catching up with each other, not necessarily proceeding in a strict chronological or logical order. Your friend tells you things aren't going very well in his job, telling you about a clash he had with his boss earlier today, and only later filling you in on the root causes of the clash that had been brewing for months. It would seem totally unnatural if he insisted on starting at the very beginning, imparting a step-by-step version of events to you.

Starting in the middle makes things much easier for you when you are communicating with a customer. You don't need to know what the ultimate story is or what you will say next. You only need to start the conversation, *Say "yes, and . . ."* as things happen, *Explore and heighten, Work with what you are given* and believe confidently that every idea is a bridge to the best idea. If you are on your customer's path, the conversation is much more likely to heighten as you explore it.

If you are on your customer's path, the conversation is much more likely to heighten as you explore it.

This reminds me of the way a flock of birds takes off from the ground as it starts a southward migration. Although the ultimate destination is south, the flock may first take off to the northwest, falling into formation and turning south only after all the birds are in sync with each other. Use the start of a conversation to get you and your customer in sync, not worrying whether you are communicating a perfect story, beginning to end. Find the path that is most comfortable for your customer, and it will be easier to move towards your desired destination.

You often have to change the course of your conversation when your customer changes the subject and takes the conversation in a different direction. Here's an example: You are taking a prospective customer on a tour of your facility. As you are walking into to your high-tech, state-of-the-art data center, preparing to introduce your vice-president of information technology who is going to explain your company's extensive data security processes, your prospective customer asks you an unrelated question about a feature of one of your products. Don't tell him to wait until you are done with the data center tour. Say "yes" to this change of course, and discuss the product feature, because you want your customer to sense that you are both in a flowing conversation that is relevant to him. Don't risk tampering with the your customer's rhythm just so you don't inconvenience your vice-president of information technology. He can wait.

Adapting to a customer's change of subject is also very important in presentations. I cringe when I hear a business person, in the middle of a PowerPoint presentation, answer an audience member's question by saying, "We'll get to that in a few slides." This makes the presenter sound like he is reciting a canned sales pitch. In order to *ditch the pitch* the presenter must take another approach.

As an example, imagine that you are presenting to a customer, introducing her to a new set of custom features available with your product. The customer says, "What does all of this customization do to our delivery times? Do we need to wait longer if we want custom features?" You've prepared a wonderful chart that illustrates the impact of customization on delivery times, but it is sitting 15 slides away in your presentation. You are left with two choices:

1. ***Shift your agenda and answer the question now.*** Your computer has an escape key, and you shouldn't be afraid to use it in a presentation. Get out of "slide show mode," navigate to your chart, and show it now. Yes, you broke the formality of the presentation, but you said "yes" to your customer. You should always shift your agenda to your customer's requests if you can.

2. ***Acknowledge the validity of the question, and postpone discussion of it until later.*** You don't want your customer to feel shut down, so you can't just say, "We'll get to that later." There is a reason he asked the question now, so look for that reason, acknowledge it as a valid question, and suggest that you'll be able to answer it fully in a few minutes. "**Yes,** of course, customization does add to our processing times, since we will need time to integrate any particular features you request into the product. We've already thought through this issue, and in a few minutes I'm going to share with you a chart that will help you decide how to balance for customization and delivery time. I can share the information now, if you like, but I think it will make more sense in a bit." Sometimes when your customer changes the subject she might make a statement that you don't agree with. When I'm in a situation like this, I tell myself that "everything my customer says is true, because my customer believes it is true."

It's hard not to be surprised and frustrated by things that customers say in persuasive conversations. You have a ten-minute conversation with a customer about your product and then he says something that reveals that he has not understood the most basic features you have been discussing. A customer uses your product for a year, reaping great benefits from it, but then reports that it is "okay." You go out of your way to help a customer, and then in the next conversation he says everything but "thanks."

Our natural inclination is to focus on how our customer is "wrong" or "doesn't get it." Well, yes, your customer may be wrong, and might not get it. But, as far as your customer is concerned, everything he says is true.

The only response you can have when your customer says something "wrong" is to accept that, although it may be wrong, it is true and is the new reality. Your customer's truth is part of the universe you share with your customer, and you must accept it. It is tempting to fight your customer's truth, denying it, arguing against it, resisting it, but that won't get you anywhere.

In one of the classes I took at Second City as research for this book, I was about to enter an improvised scene where one of my classmates was playing a person ordering a ton of food at McDonald's. I was preparing to join the scene, thinking I could play her doctor, catching her in the act of being a fast food junkie. Then she announced to the person playing the cashier that she had just been rescued off of a deserted island and this was her first day back in civilization.

She had just redefined the "truth." She was no longer the fast-food junkie I thought she was. She was someone tasting cooked food for the first time in years. I couldn't be her doctor anymore, so I quickly shifted course and entered the scene as the person who had rescued her from the deserted island.

My classmate's announcement that she had just been rescued off of a desert island may seem like a pretty extreme shift of reality, but customers will often redefine the truth in similarly extreme ways. "Our budget was just slashed," or "We're making Janice the project manager," or "The project has been put on hold for three months" are scene-changers. It's really tempting to be frustrated by these kinds of situations, but the fact remains: your customer has redefined a new truth. Similar to the way I had immediately change my approach when my classmate defined a new reality, you will often have to accept new truths that your customers put in front of you, no matter how unexpected or "wrong" they are.

These redefinitons of the truth aren't always bad, of course. Today a client said to me, "Steve, we've had some personnel changes and are having challenges with senior management buy-off, so how much will it cost to extend your contract for one more month?" Personnel changes and senior management bureaucracy have become the new truth in their organization, and my best course of action is to recognize that truth and work with it.

If you focus on denying and resisting your customer's truth, you won't be able to see a clear way out of this truth to a better place. Let's imagine that a customer says that she thinks a competitor's product is as good as yours, but you know with 100 percent certainty that your product will work better for her than the competitor's. Should you focus on the fact that she is wrong, or focus on understanding her version of the truth? What will make it easier for you to deal with the situation and eventually encourage her to embrace a new version of the truth?

When your customer says something you don't like, say "yes" to the new reality. Recognize your customer's truth. Then you will be in a much better position to help your customer shift from her current idea of what is true to a different truth.

RECAP: Find Your Customer's Path

Don't force a conversation's direction on your customer. See what path will make it easiest for your customer to fall into a flowing conversation with you. Focus on getting the conversation moving, and on getting a good conversational flow between you and your customer.

*   *   *

🌀 PRACTICE: Get Rid of Your But

Earlier we discussed the practice *Say "Yes, and..."* to help you *Create a series of "yeses."* One mistake people often make is to respond with "yes, but" instead of "yes, and." When you say "but," it prevents you from heightening a conversation.

Consider this: If one actor on stage improvises the line, "Let's go bobsledding standing on our heads," and another actor says, "**Yes**, that would be fun, **but** it would be dangerous," the audience is going to feel that the scene has stalled.

What if the other actor had responded with, "**Yes**, that would be fun, **and** I'll dial 911 before we go down the hill, so the ambulance will be on its way even before we crash!" Much more entertaining.

Let's explore how this works in a persuasive conversation. Recently I was coaching a salesperson who sells high-end men's clothing to help him prepare for a persuasive conversation with a retailer. Due to the tough economy, this retailer was threatening to reduce the amount of this salesperson's product his stores carried. Role-playing as the retail buyer, I said, "Our customers have less money to spend, and we don't think they are willing to pay for your kind of product. So we're going to cut back and only carry a few of your pieces this season."

Trying to use the concept of *Saying "Yes, and,"* the salesperson's role-playing response was, "**Yes**, I agree that your customers have less money to spend, so they are being very careful with their dollars. **But** we could focus this season on the lowest-priced items in our line, so you won't lose the customers who come into your store looking for our merchandise."

I asked him to rephrase his comment, using the word "and" instead of "but." Here's what he came up with: "**Yes**, I agree that your customers have less money to spend, so they are being very careful with their dollars. **And** I think that we can find a way to keep most of those scarce dollars in your stores. We share customers who are loyal to your brand and to mine, and we don't want to lose that loyalty. So if we focus this season on my lower-priced items, we can protect our customer relationships in this tough time."

Although both answers communicate essentially the same message, the salesperson's second response will be much more effective. In the first response, the salesperson is disagreeing with his customer by saying "but." By *Getting rid of his but* in the second response, he is able to build on what his customer says. "Yes, but" slows a conversation down, while "Yes, and" moves a conversation forward.

Also, notice how "and" helped this salesperson build on his own idea. After saying "but," he said his idea could help the retailer retain his customers. However, after saying "and," he naturally offered a much richer, more interesting, more positive way of saying the same thing. Saying "and" doesn't only move the conversation forward for your customer, it moves the conversation forward for you.

So *Get rid of your but.* It will help you *Explore and heighten.*

RECAP: Get Rid of Your "But"

"Yes, but" equals "No"

"But" stops conversations.

"And" keeps conversations flowing.

Practice keeping the "but" out of your persuasive conversations.

*   *   *

🌀 PRACTICE: Make Accidents Work

In improvisation, actors learn to embrace the possibilities that 'accidents' offer. Experience shows them that some of the most powerful and compelling work comes out of accidents on stage, in large part because everyone—actors and audience—is engaged by the heightened drama that unfolds when something completely unpredictable occurs.[30]

—TOM YORTON

Though she has celebrated her 85th birthday, my aunt, Roslyn Alexander, can still be seen in Chicago stage productions, earning rave reviews. She was recently in a production called *Jacob and Jack* at the Victory Gardens Theater in Chicago, in which she played the mother of a young actress. In one scene, Roz's character barges into a dressing room just as a famous actor is trying to seduce her daughter. In each performance, Roz's character displays angry emotions, screaming at both the offending actor and her rebellious daughter. One evening, Roz got a nosebleed just as this scene was starting. Unable to stop the bleeding, she went onstage holding a tissue to her nose. To make sense of the tissue she was holding to her nose, she made a quick decision to play the scene as though she were crying into a tissue because of what was happening to her daughter. The other two actors, Craig Spidle, playing the actor, and Laura Scheinbaum, playing Roz's daughter, each saw what was happening, and said "yes" to the new situation, adapting their characters' reactions to reflect the different emotions Roz brought to the stage this night. They both said "yes" and worked with Roz to make the accident work. (Yes, even in a scripted stage production there is room for improvisation.)

Accidents happen frequently in improvised shows. In a recent performance by the improv group Chicagoland at the Annoyance Theater, a drunk audience member started shouting things from his seat. One of the actors fell to the floor and said, "I'm hearing voices in my head." T.J. Jagadowski, a prominent Chicago improv actor, said, "Let's see what we can do to get the voices in your head to shut the &*%@ up." The audience burst into laughter and applause. The actors effectively worked with this accident until the "accident" disappeared, i.e., until the Annoyance staff escorted the intoxicated audience member to the door.

Making accidents work in persuasive conversations is critical, since accidents will inevitably happen. You or your customer will at some point write down the wrong time for a meeting. One of you will spill coffee at lunch. Cell phone calls with customers will drop at inconvenient times. I once had a pen start leaking all over my hand in a client's finely appointed conference room. No matter what happens, short of someone suffering bodily harm or someone making a cruelly offensive remark, you can always find a way to make an accident work.

The trick to making accidents work is to remember a principle we introduced earlier: Every idea is a bridge to the best idea. You must believe that, no matter what happens, "you can get there from here." Don't focus on the accident; focus on where you can go once the accident has happened. Everyone encounters (or creates) accidents. The trick is in what you do with them.

A corollary of *Make accidents work* is this fundamental principle of improvisation: There are no mistakes.

> *Improvisation is the ultimate disposable art form . . . Try not to be tied to any one moment or discovery.*[31]
>
> —SECOND CITY ALMANAC OF IMPROVISATION

Some accidents happen to you. Some are your own creation. One of the most comforting improvisation rules to remember is that there are no mistakes.

Halfway through a show I recently saw at the iO Theater in Chicago, an actor named Bill Arnett introduced a series of improv scenes by saying, "One of the things we always tell ourselves as improvisers is that there are no mistakes." Bill explained that improvisers gain a powerful freedom from this idea, and said, "Let's see what happens when actors aren't afraid to make mistakes." The troupe came back out onstage and began to throw crazy, outlandish ideas into their scenes, as if they were making purposeful mistakes. In every case, the other actors worked with the "mistakes," saying "yes" to them by building their reactions around them. In every case, they were able to use the mistake as a launching point from which to create a new thread in the scene.

As I mentioned earlier, music producer Yossi Fine says that he looks at unexpected occurrences as a chance to improvise and be creative. "Most of humanity's inventions were mistakes," Yossi said as he laughed and told me about how some of the most magical moments he's created on artists' records were not in his original plans. "My feeling is this: there are no mistakes, only situations."

Creativity can be messy. As Anne Libera said during our interview, "If you're Michelangelo and you're worried about making marble dust, you won't create the David."

The idea that there are no mistakes is one of the most difficult improvisation concepts for people to translate from the stage to persuasive conversations. "Of course there are mistakes I can make in a persuasive conversation!" you might say.

There are no mistakes, only situations.
—YOSSI FINE

Sure, there are deadly mistakes you can make. You can get caught daydreaming while your customer is talking, or you can call your customer by the wrong name. You might lecture your customer if you disagree with something he says. Those are certainly real mistakes.

But if you are willing to employ the habits taught here, and to learn from this rule of stage improvisation, you will understand that there are far fewer mistakes possible in a persuasive conversation than you previously thought. Many things you might think of as mistakes will not kill your conversation if you employ some of the principles we've been discussing: *Work with what you are given, Make accidents work,* and every idea is a bridge to the best idea. Go with your mistakes! Don't let them stop you in your tracks.

Instead, feel the freedom of knowing that there is never only one possibility at any point in a persuasive conversation, but many possibilities. No matter what happens to you, or no matter what mistake you make, accept it, say "yes" to it, and you will be able to move the conversation forward.

RECAP: Make Accidents Work

In the spirit of "work with what you are given," don't let unforeseen occurrences shake you. Make accidents work by accepting them as the new reality, and looking for new paths in the new realities accidents create.

*   *   *

A persuasive conversation is a process, not a presentation. In order to persuade, you have to move that conversation forward.

A persuasive conversation can't move forward unless both you and your customer collaborate to move it forward. By *Creating a series of "yeses,"* you gain your customer's collaboration, tacitly, without ever having to ask for it specifically. Mutual agreement works magically to keep a conversation flowing. By *Exploring and heightening* the conversation, you lay the foundation for persuasion.

6

Let a Shared Story Emerge Through Your Conversation

HOW TO CREATE A SHARED STORY

One of the key principles we have discussed in this book is that your customer cares **much** more about his own story than he cares about your story. Because of this, pitching your story is not the best way to persuade a customer to do business with you.

We have also discussed the importance of hearing your customer's story. A customer will appreciate if you understand his story, but even this is not enough to give a customer a reason to do business with you.

Your challenge when communicating with a customer is to evolve from "your story" and "my story" to "our story."

"Our story" is a shared story, created collaboratively through mutual discovery, in which your customer comes to see you as integral to his own story. Let's explore a few examples:

You are a financial advisor:

Client thinks about "your story."

When a customer thinks about you, he thinks about your office, your credentials, and the products you sell.

Client thinks about "our story."

When your client thinks of his retirement, he can't help but think of the plans and strategies you have created together, and of how your capabilities have made it all happen. The story of his retirement planning is a story in which both of you figure prominently.

You are a dentist who has just finished a long process of reconstructive implants for a patient:

Patient thinks of "your story."

The patient uses words like "proficient" and "highly satisfied" if someone asks him about you.

Patient thinks "our story."

The patient is incredibly impressed with your skills, but when he talks of the experience with his friends he talks about so much more, referring continually to the way you counseled him through the process and helped him make decisions about his best course of treatment.

You are a veterinarian:

Customer thinks "your story."

The pet owner says, "The vet put my dog to sleep."

Customer thinks "our story."

"We made the best choice for Fido's comfort."

You are a product photographer:

Customer thinks "your story."

"He took nice pictures of our products."

Customer thinks "our story."

"We really were able to show our products in their best light and increase sales."

This idea of creating "our story" is the central theme of my book *We: The Ideal Customer Relationship*. The concept of "We" was something I observed empirically. In market research my consulting firm conducted, we noticed that customers who were most passionate about a company used "We" language, i.e., they often spoke in the first person plural when describing the company, product or service in question. "Frank was great. We came up with a strong plan for our retirement." Or, "Betty is the best wedding planner imaginable. We put on an amazing, memorable wedding." When customers perceived a shared story, resulting in a "We" relationship, it is difficult for them to describe a business without describing their connection to that business.

Improv actors create shared stories by involving the audience in the performance at different times. The most common example of this is when improvisers ask for an audience suggestion. My cousin Debbie and I saw an improvised musical at the Studio Be Theater in Chicago recently. At the start of the show, the pianist dragged her fingers across the keys from the high register down to the low register, instructing the audience to yell "stop" while she did it. This led to her stopping on a "B" note, after which one of the actors yelled out, "Give us a name that starts with a B." Debbie yelled out "Beatrice," and for the next hour, the heroine of the story used the name given by Debbie. Similar audience suggestions led to the musical being set in England, Beatrice having a best friend who had long fingernails and was into punk music, and Beatrice having a boyfriend named Percy. Through a simple device, the actors made the audience feel part of the story.

Matt Hovde of Second City says that when the audience feels part of the story, "they are desperate to see you succeed." Wouldn't it be wonderful if, through the creation of a shared story, your customer becomes desperate to see you succeed?

Let's explore specific habits and practices you can use to let a shared story emerge through your conversations with your customers.

HABIT #5

Focus the Conversation on Your Customer

SCENE: The salesperson is still charged up from last week's national sales meeting. At this meeting, he learned that his company has just introduced a fabulous line of new products that improve the existing product line. He can't wait to share this exciting news with his customers, and today's sales call is his first chance to do so. He walks into his customer's office, so excited he can barely stand it, and, shortly after the meeting starts he launches into an enthusiastic description of the new products. He is equipped with sell sheets, charts, a brand new Power-Point presentation, and order forms, all of which he shows to the customer. He's expecting the customer to share his enthusiasm for the new products, but instead, the customer begins fidgeting in his chair and fiddling with his pen. The salesperson finishes his presentation, and the customer says, "So, what else you got?"

You may be very excited about the story you have to communicate to your customer, but this doesn't mean that your customer will be excited by your story. You have a much better chance of engaging your customer if you focus on his story, not on your story.

"What?" you may ask. "How can I persuade if I don't talk about what I'm selling, or about the issue I'm trying to persuade someone to agree with?"

The answer: Make sure the conversation is about your customer, and carefully weave tidbits about you, your company and your products into this conversation.

As discussed at the beginning of this book, one of the most fundamental reasons to *ditch the pitch* is that our customers really don't care about our stories. They care about their own stories *much* more than they care about our stories.

Make the sure the conversation is about your customer.

Every person you see, everywhere and at all times, has a personal narrative going on in his or her head at the time you see them. These personal narratives revolve around stories such as "what I am doing," "what's important to me right now," "who I am with," and, of course, "who I am." Every person, except maybe the most peaceful yogi on the top of a mountain, has a narrative going on in his or her mind, at this very moment, that describes the situation of his or her life.

This is, of course, true for your customer. Your customer enters a persuasive conversation with you, whether this is the 1st or 1001st time you've met together, with a story already happening in her mind. She knows what brought her to you, she knows (or at least thinks she knows) what she wants, and she has an ongoing background narrative about her situation playing in her head. She is holding on tightly to her story as you start talking, and you must be very careful not to knock this story out of her hands. Ensure that your conversation stays focused on her story, and you will be much more likely to keep her engaged in your persuasive conversation.

One of the best ways to help a customer become engaged in conversation with you is empathic listening. By listening to what she has to say, and acknowledging that you hear it, she will be more drawn to you and the conversation. In a sales setting, "What's in it for me?" is at the top of every customer's mind, so if you want someone to be engaged, keep the conversation focused on them. People want to know they are being heard and listening is one of the best ways to say "yes."

> *Ensure that your conversation stays focused on her story, and you will be much more likely to keep her engaged in your persuasive conversation.*

A study by R.B van Baaren, et. al., of the University of Nijmegen in the Netherlands, shows the value of demonstrating to customers that you have heard what they have to say. In this study, which was published in the *Journal of Experimental Social Psychology*,[32] restaurant servers earned significantly higher tips when they repeated customers' orders back to them. Van Baaren and his team described research where restaurant customers were divided into two groups. For the first group, servers repeated customers' orders back to them, and for the second group, servers took the orders without repeating them. All other variables were of course controlled as well as possible. The customers who heard their orders repeated left tips that were 68 percent higher than the customers who did not hear their orders repeated. If waiters receive this magnitude of a tip premium just by repeating back restaurant orders, imagine how much more your customers will value you if you acknowledge and validate their stories. Let's explore how.

🌀 PRACTICE: Make 95% of the Conversation about Your Customer

A few weeks ago I had the chance to meet with a company's management team to discuss the possibility of working with them on a major strategic project. The president of the company had invited me to meet his team, gathering us together for a lunch in their conference room. He started the meeting with a very flattering introduction, explaining to his team why he wanted them to meet me. After the introduction, he turned to me and said, "Steve, why don't you tell everyone about yourself and your company, and what kinds of other clients you work with."

All eyes were on me, with everyone looking eager to hear me speak. On the surface, this seemed like a great moment for a consultant like me who is trying to sell his services: the boss has just told his team great things about me, and the team was keen to hear my message. So the best thing for me to do was seize this opportunity and tell this willing audience about my credentials, and how my qualifications make me perfectly qualified to help them, right? Wrong.

Oh, I was tempted. But I knew it was the wrong thing to do.

The worst thing I could have done was to launch into a story about myself. No matter how interested everyone in the room was, I knew their interest would wane if I began talking about Yastrow & Company. Even if I were extremely captivating, it would take no more than thirty seconds before people started thinking about their next meeting, a phone call they needed to make, or the homework assignment they were going to help their child with that evening.

I resisted the temptation to tell my story, knowing that the best way to hold their attention was to talk about them. Instead of launching into a description of my company and how we could help them, I said, "Thanks, I'd love to tell you about Yastrow & Company. First, if you don't mind, I'd like to hear about you, so I can be sure to tell you things about us that are most relevant to your situation." Then I began a dialogue that turned into a very productive ninety-minute conversation about their business.

The good news: In the entire ninety minutes I never had to talk about Yastrow & Company.

Yes, I did manage to communicate many important points about my company and myself throughout the meeting. But every time I said something about my company or about myself, I made sure that the conversation was really still about their company and their issues, demonstrating to them that I understood and had empathy for their situation and was listening carefully to what they had to say. I was careful to make every statement about Yastrow & Company brief and to connect each piece of information about myself to something about their company. For example: "I saw a similar situation with another client, and here's how we approached it," or, "I understand the challenge you've just described. What I would suggest is . . ."

That I never had to tell a complete story about my company, my services, or myself helped make this a very effective persuasive conversation and a very successful sales call. I introduced small nuggets of my story into the conversation about their business, and every piece of information about me was connected to a part of their story. Not only did they learn about me in that ninety minutes, they understood how my capabilities connected directly to their needs. (Yes, in case you are curious, I was awarded the project.)

At every moment, in every customer conversation, continually ask yourself, "Are we still talking about them?" If you notice that the conversation has drifted from being a conversation about the customer to a conversation about you or what you are trying to sell, change course, now! Don't let the conversation turn into a conversation about what you are selling, because the customer really doesn't want to hear it, even if he is pretending he wants to hear it. He wants to hear about himself. If you notice that the conversation is about you, change it! *Focus the conversation on your customer.*

Here's a number I keep in my head during persuasive conversations: 95%.

I focus on keeping 95% of the conversation about the customer. What this means is that I have a very small ration of time allotted to talking about what I am selling. While my customer and I might both speak an equal amount, I focus on making sure that 95% of the subject matter is about them. Therefore, anytime the topic of conversation focuses on my company, my products or my services, I know that I need to swing it back to a focus on the customer as quickly as possible. I must use that 5% wisely. Once again, returning to the story related above about my meeting with the CEO and his team, I used this idea that 95% of the conversation should be about the customer as a rule of thumb to keep the conversation on track. Each time I found myself talking about myself, I knew I needed to return the conversation quickly back to a conversation about the customer.

It's this simple: You can't be *ditching the pitch* if you are talking about what you are trying to sell. So ensure that, 95% of the time, the conversation should be about your customer.

> ## RECAP: Make 95% of the Conversation about Your Customer
>
> Always monitor how much of the conversation is about your customer's situation and how much is about you or what you are offering. Ensure that 95% is about your customer.

*   *   *

🐝 PRACTICE: Obey the One-Paragraph Rule

How long are you able to pay attention when someone starts a monologue? How much do you enjoy listening to someone who talks too much? And have you ever caught yourself talking too much?

Most people stop listening when another person talks too much. It's easy to get distracted and start thinking about other things when someone babbles on in a monologue.

Whenever I discuss this in my workshops, audience members are virtually unanimous in their disgust with "monologuers." Yet, most of these same people admit that they often fall into the monologue trap themselves, especially on the job.

Does it really matter? Is it possible that monologues, while irritating, don't really have an impact on business outcomes? Could a monologue be like a television commercial, a distracting nuisance, whose message we ignore, but hardly enough of a reason to give up watching your favorite show?

No. Monologues destroy sales conversations. If you are monologuing, your customer is spacing out. He's thinking of something else. He's not enjoying himself.

So, what do we do?

My brother Phil sells very complex "application-specific integrated circuits" for Avago Technologies, a Hewlett-Packard spin-off, and he often has to explain highly complicated information to customers. Knowing that this is the kind of situation that can lead to excessive monologues, Phil came up with a very useful tool called **"The One-Paragraph Rule."**

Here's how it works: When you are speaking with a customer, try never to give more than one paragraph's worth of information without a break. Just as a book has a short break between paragraphs, allow some space after each chunk of information that you deliver. This gives your customer a chance to say something, ask a question, or absorb what you are saying. And, equally important, it gives you a chance to read your customer's reactions.

This gives your customer a chance to:

- Speak

- Acknowledge she understands you

- Signal that she doesn't understand you

- Show you that she is interested

- Show you that she is not interested

Alex von Bidder says that he teaches his people at New York's Four Seasons Restaurant to "minimize the monologue" in a way that is very similar to the One-Paragraph Rule. "The number of specials we tell customers about is really crucial. People lose interest after hearing about a few, so we try not to have more than that. And, if you mention too many ingredients when describing a dish you get yourself into trouble. Just because you have ten ingredients you don't need to talk about every one." Amen.

The one-paragraph rule isn't always easy to obey. We have a lot to say, and we've been trained to believe that sales and marketing are about telling stories to our customers. It takes a lot of discipline and a lot of "un-learning," to stop talking.

But, learning to practice the one-paragraph rule is really worth it.

I remember my first experiences selling. I was a summer intern at MTI Vacations in Oak Brook, IL, between my first and second year of MBA study at Northwestern University's J.L. Kellogg Graduate School of Management. After a few weeks on the job I was on an airplane to Hawaii to sell advertising in MTI's Hawaii vacation brochures. I had no idea what I was doing, and I used every sales call as a chance to present my case. I was totally focused on giving my pitch and, after I gave it, I waited to hear the customer's response. Needless to say, I didn't do very well. If only I had known about the one-paragraph rule.

Fast-forward twenty years . . . A few months ago I had a phone call with the owner of a company that was making a decision about hiring Yastrow & Company for a consulting project. I'd been dealing with the company's president, and this was my first chance to speak with his boss, the owner. I knew I had to impress him because he was going to play a role in the decision to hire my company.

As we started talking, it was clear that he was very eager to tell me about the company, and he began to relate some very interesting stories to me. After fifteen minutes, we still hadn't talked about Yastrow & Company or my project proposal. I wasn't worried about this, but I knew, based on what the company's president had told me, that I had to communicate some key points during the call if I wanted the owner to support my proposal.

Finally, there was a chance for me to speak. *Obeying the one-paragraph rule*, I said a small bit of information that responded to what he'd been talking about, and then paused to leave some space. It was tempting to disregard the rule, since I had a lot more to communicate, and limited time to communicate it, but as if Phil's voice were in my ear coaching me, I stopped talking.

The owner jumped back in, taking this opportunity to speak for a few more minutes. When he stopped, I commented on what he said and then paused, after which he talked some more. This lopsided back and forth went on for a while. I only spoke every few minutes, but I was very careful to ensure that I didn't talk too long each time that I spoke, and I also made sure that what I said was based on what he was saying. Slowly but surely, one small paragraph at a time, I managed to weave my important selling points into the conversation.

As this was happening, I imagined myself twenty years ago. I would have been nervous, concerned that I was missing my opportunity to tell my story. I would have stored up all the things I wanted to say, and I would have spit them all out at once as soon as I had a chance, as if to balance the score in the conversation. Fortunately, I've gained some patience and discipline as I've gained experience. I knew that this conversation was going very well, even though I hadn't said much. I knew that my goal wasn't to tell him everything about me. My goal was to have a conversation with him that made him want to have more conversations with me.

The conversation did go well. Even though he didn't hear my entire story, he felt good enough about the conversation to give a "thumbs-up" to the company president, and Yastrow & Company won the project.

Practice the one-paragraph rule in every conversation you have and you will find that it becomes second nature. If you start talking too long ... you will notice.

RECAP: Obey the One-Paragraph Rule

Never speak more than one paragraph's worth of information at one time without leaving a break. During that break try to read your customer, allow them a chance to say something, and give yourself a chance to modify the course of the conversation based on what happens.

*   *   *

🌑 PRACTICE: Weave Your Stories Together

One of the major themes in learning to *ditch the pitch* is that your customer cares much more about his story than about your story, and therefore, you want to keep the conversation focused on his story. In order to help your customer see, for himself, why working with you is a good idea for him, you want to gently weave the threads of your story into your customer's story. Don't miss the word "gently" in the previous sentence; in order to keep the conversation focused on your customer's story (what he really cares about), you need to be very careful, at all points in the conversation, not to overpower your customer's story with your own. Like an embroiderer carefully weaving a beautiful pattern into a fabric, you want to enrich your customer's story without overshadowing it. Your goal is to weave those elements into your customer's story, at appropriate times.

For example, let's say you are an architect meeting a prospective client for the first time. There are many things that you would like him to learn about you, such as your experience with buildings of the kind he wants to build, your capabilities for designing ecologically sustainable yet economical buildings, the strength of your team, the strong level of client satisfaction you have created, and the high level of aesthetic sensibilities that you believe you bring to your designs. There is no way a person meeting you for the first time could absorb all of these details in one conversation, so you can't even try to communicate this entire story.

Instead, you gently weave the right piece of the story into the conversation at the right time. There may be an appropriate time to discuss aesthetics, and another time to discuss the strength of your team. By disaggregating your story into its component threads, and then weaving these threads into his story at the right times, you can integrate information about you, your products, and your company into the conversation without distracting the main focus of the conversation from your customer.

RECAP: Weave Your Stories Together

As your conversation continues and centers on your customer, look for opportunities to weave small pieces of your story (gently) into your customer's story. At all times remember that your objective is not to focus on your story but to create "our story."

*   *   *

HABIT #6
Don't Rush the Story

SCENE: The salesperson listens patiently as the prospective customer describes her situation. Being the quick study that he is, the salesperson figures out a perfect solution for this customer in the first two minutes after the customer starts talking. The next few minutes reinforce the salesperson's ideas, and he is getting very excited to tell his customer about his solution.

Finally, after about five minutes, the salesperson can wait no longer. With enthusiasm and confidence, he lays out a complete, perfect plan for the customer to address every one of her problems. He describes his company's capabilities, creating a very solid, reasoned, rational argument about how these capabilities are perfectly suited to the customer's issues.

When he finishes talking, he looks to the customer expecting approval for coming up with such a brilliant solution in so little time. But, instead of applauding, the customer says, "I don't know. That sounds like an awful lot."

As we saw earlier, good stage improvisers don't force a story into a scene before the scene is ready for the story. They focus on character and context, and have the patience to let the story develop as the scene unfolds. Matt Hovde of Second City says, "It is important not to 'railroad' somebody, forcing them to follow your story choices. As an improviser, it is extremely frustrating to be in a scene where someone is ignoring everything you are saying and doing because they are forcing their agenda."

> *It is important not to 'railroad' somebody, forcing them to follow your story choices.*

The same holds true in a persuasive conversation; it is very important not to force the story before its time.

In a sales pitch a salesperson proclaims, "Here is the story I want to tell you. This is the information I want us to focus on." Is it not surprising that customers often feel overwhelmed by sales pitches? But in a persuasive conversation, the story emerges gradually, and this feels very comfortable to the customer.

Don't force the perfect story

The best ideas never spill out of people's minds in their final, finished form. When creative ideas first see the light of day, they are usually rough likenesses of their eventual selves. Great ideas are developed through a series of iterations.

What this means is that creators of ideas spend a lot of time working with unfinished ideas that are far from perfect. Similarly, it's okay to be in a conversation with a customer not knowing exactly what the best outcome is, or the best offering for this customer, or what this customer really wants. It's okay to be in a conversation with a customer not having determined the right way to sell this customer. The entire process of the persuasive conversation is designed to figure these things out, and you shouldn't worry if you don't have all the answers while you are in the middle of a sales conversation. A persuasive conversation is a process, not a presentation.

Don't force the perfect story. Let the story evolve during your persuasive conversation, paying attention to the emerging story at each point in its development. Don't rush it.

I use this principle in every persuasive conversation I have. I sell a highly varied and customizable set of consulting services, and every company benefits from my work in a different way. I can't possibly know the right approach for any one prospective client until I have spoken with that client for a while, which means I end up spending lots of time talking with my future clients without knowing the story I want them to understand. During this time I rely on the story-in-progress, working with it as it develops into the right story for each client.

> *A persuasive conversation is a process, not a presentation.*

The temptation for most salespeople is to say too much too soon. A salesperson needs to avoid what Rich Sheridan, Sales Vice-President for salesforce.com calls "premature elaboration."

No matter how compelling your story is, or how amazing your insights are, you will not get credit for compelling-ness and amazing-ness if you bring your ideas forth too quickly. You need the patience to wait to communicate certain things, because your customer may not be ready to hear them.

Wait... wait... wait... keep waiting... and never jump the gun by bringing something into the conversation before its time. Don't worry. You will know when it is time, especially if you are alert and paying attention to what is going on. Patience is one of the best virtues a successful persuader can have. Let the conversation develop. Nurture the conversation and gently guide it in the right direction, without forcing topics into it.

Don't write the end of the scene before its time

*My improv students sometimes tell me how they plan to end
a scene. I say, 'you have no idea what's going to happen, and
if you try to make it go there you're going to miss.'*

—Matt Hovde

Although you may have goals in a persuasive conversation, it is dangerous to pre-determine the specific way a persuasive conversation is going to end. As a persuasive conversation progresses, you will (if you are practicing the habits described here,) discover new avenues down which you can escort your customer through the conversation. If you are open to every possibility, you may see an even better, more appropriate ending point for a conversation than you could have possibly conceived of ahead of time.

Don't rush the story, and don't determine the end of a given sales conversation before it has even begun.

🌀 PRACTICE: Don't Load the Slingshot

I was recently coaching a salesperson who sells a stress-relief program for overworked professionals, such as lawyers, accountants, and doctors. We were role-playing, and I was pretending to be a potential customer, a stressed-out lawyer who was working too much, barely able to bear the stress.

The salesperson asked me a few questions about my situation, which I answered by describing my intense stress, and then he launched into a perfectly logical explanation of everything he could do for me:

"I can see what kind of stress you are under, so let me tell you about our programs to deal with that kind of stress. We offer a complete program, including chiropractic services, relaxation techniques, massage therapy, stress counseling, and a complete website so you can access stress-relief tools whenever you want. We believe that for people like you, we should start with a twelve-week program, where you would visit us three times a week and also be able to call in any time you feel stressed. Our methods are proven and have been shown to make a major difference in people's lives. I can give you the phone numbers of people who've been through our program, so you can hear from them how effective it is."

My advice to the salesperson: "Everything you just said makes logical sense and speaks to my needs, but as a customer, you just lost me. I'm playing the role of an overworked lawyer, about to burst. I'm under so much stress and pressure, and my character is in a very emotional state. After hearing about my situation and gathering your facts, you immediately started talking about your product. I still want us to talk about me! You're overloading me with all sorts of information I'm not ready to hear."

Since this salesperson has spent a lot of time thinking about how he can help people similar to the character I was playing, it's not surprising that he immediately thought of and diagnosed a solution for me. But he made the mistake of putting his entire story into a metaphorical slingshot, pulling back on the sling, aiming it at me, and letting it fly all at once.

Ditching the pitch isn't only about abandoning your pre-written sales pitch and developing a sales story on the spot as you learn about your customer. It is also about communicating that story through a fresh, spontaneous, collaborative dialogue with your customer. If you *load the slingshot* and bombard your customer with your entire prescription for how you can help him, all at once, you will not create a spontaneous, collaborative dialogue. You will knock him over.

Carl Tominberg, a very successful labor and employment attorney in Chicago, has had excellent sales success throughout his career. In a sales workshop I was running for the firm's attorneys, one of the young attorneys said, "I have a hard time explaining to people what I do as a lawyer. It's pretty technical, and by the time I finish describing it, I've usually confused the person I'm speaking with."

In response, Carl said, "If someone asks me what I do, I just say that I'm a lawyer. I don't offer any details. Then they usually ask me to tell them more. At that point, they are interested because they have asked a question they want an answer to, so I can give them some more information."

Here's what you need to do: Tear up your sales pitch into little pieces. But don't throw the pieces away.

Save them. And plan to use them a little at a time.

Think of these pieces as individual *threads* of your story, which you will be able to weave into your customer's story, creating a shared story, one piece at a time, without overwhelming your customer or hijacking the conversation.

> ## RECAP: Don't Load the Slingshot
>
> Because you "know your stuff," you may, during a persuasive conversation, quickly think of many things you could tell your customer. Resist the temptation to tell your customers all of those things, all at once. Don't load the slingshot!

*   *   *

🌀 PRACTICE: Leave Things in Your Pocket

I have seen, yet quickly forgotten, movies with elaborate sets and multi-million dollar special effects budgets. I have also seen plays with very sparse sets that have moved me to tears, creating indelible imprints in my mind that I will never forget. The most powerful improvisation scenes I have ever seen have been between two actors on a stage with nothing but chairs to describe their physical environment. When it comes to effective communication, less is often more.

In the previous practice, *Don't load the slingshot*, we discussed the importance of not telling your customer too much at one time. But that doesn't mean that you should *eventually* tell your customer everything. The opposite is true. There is much that you should never tell your customer.

The goal of a persuasive conversation is not to tell your customer everything you could possibly tell her. Your goal is to earn the right to continue the conversation so you can persuade her, and that is *always* best served by *not* telling your customer everything you could possibly tell her.

One of the biggest mistakes I have seen salespeople make is to force-fit information into a conversation because they think the customer "should" hear it. "They need to know we have offices in twenty-seven countries," or "They should know that we've been in business since 1965." Why? Unless the salesperson has learned, through persuasive conversation, that these pieces of information are important to the customer, he should *Leave them in his pocket.*

One of the great ironies of human communication is that words can get in the way of effective communication. The more you tell your customer, the more chance there is to overwhelm her, disinterest her, or lose her attention.

Earlier, I discussed the practice of *Saying less to notice more.* If you say less, in addition to giving yourself the opportunity to notice more, your customer will also notice more.

RECAP: Leave Things in Your Pocket

Remember that your goal is not to tell you customer everything you could tell her. It is to move a conversation forward and eventually persuade her. Resist the temptation to tell your customer everything you could. Too much information gets in the way . . . leave things in your pocket.

*   *   *

PRACTICE: Create Callbacks

We're always listening, remembering, and recycling.
—CHARNA HALPERN

How does it feel to you when a person makes reference to things you said previously? What does it make you feel about her ability to help you?

Watch any good comedy, whether it is improvised or scripted, and you will see many recurring references throughout a show. Watch the audience members' reactions as these references return, and you will notice that they laugh more each time. What's up with that? These returning ideas are called "callbacks," which are references to statements or ideas presented earlier, often heightened or developed each time they return.

Let's explore why callbacks are so effective in comedy in order to understand why they are so effective in persuasive conversations. There are three main reasons callbacks work.

First, when the audience recognizes a callback, they feel like they're in on the joke. Their laughs get louder with each successive callback of an idea because they feel like they're on the inside, in cahoots with the team onstage. They are "with" the cast, not just watching the cast. That's why applause in comedy shows is much more like cheering in a sporting event than it is like the clapping in a classical music concert. In the concert you are paying respect to the virtuosity and artistry of the musician. In the comedy show or sporting event you are exclaiming, "Yeah, we did it!!"

Second, a callback ties material together, making it easier to understand and engage with that material. I saw a performance of Susan Messing's show *Messing with a Friend* last week, in which her "friend" for that performance was T.J. Jagadowski. Susan started the show by asking for a suggestion, and an audience member yelled out "tennis balls." Susan and T.J. immediately improvised a hilarious scene as two people playing tennis. Halfway through the show, about five improvised scenes later, they played a completely different couple shopping for tennis balls at Sports Authority. Near the end of the show they returned as the original couple on the tennis court. The tennis theme acted like a thread that tied an unrelated group of scenes together into one show.

Mick Napier explains that a callback is "a built-in recollection of the truth that is presented to people." Tying material together adds coherence and resonance, making ideas more believable to both theater audiences and customers.

Third, callbacks show the audience—or a customer—that you are listening to them. Improv actors typically start a show by asking for an audience suggestion. The person who yelled out "tennis balls" had the honor of knowing that Susan and T.J. listened to him, and as we know, human beings love to be heard.

When an audience—or customers—see the story forming in the moment, out of the what's-happening-right-now-right-in-front-of-us, they feel part of it. They feel engaged. They feel listened to.

When you engage your customers with callbacks during persuasive conversations, you aren't rewarded with laughs. You are rewarded with something more important: attention and interest.

Imagine you and your spouse have spent the last four Saturday afternoons touring houses with a realtor, hoping to find a new home for your family. You have seen about fifteen homes and throughout the process the realtor has learned many things about your interests and needs. By this point the realtor isn't talking about the individual houses you are seeing. Each time you see a new living room, kitchen, master suite, or backyard she is able to relate it to what you have already seen and what your impressions were. "This backyard is even better for you than the one we saw on Victor Court. Joey can actually find a place to put third base that isn't right by your kitchen window," referencing a story you told her about a throw that was aimed too high, shattered glass, and became the reason your son isn't getting his allowance this month. Or, "This kitchen is no good for you. You've said many times that you want more prep space and easy access to the dining room."

Wouldn't these references to interests and concerns you've indicated in previous conversations make you feel more interested and engaged in what the realtor had to say? Wouldn't the realtor's callbacks make you feel like she has taken the time to understand your particular needs and that she's giving you all of her attention?

A major reason that we need to *ditch the pitch* is that it is very difficult to get and hold customers' attention in our noisy, modern world. People are bombarded with thousands of persuasive messages every day, and their lives are overly crowded with noise, priorities, and demands. If you are in business, it's a miracle that a customer even remembers the name of your company, let alone becomes emotionally engaged with your business and its products. *Creating callbacks* is one of the best ways to hold a customer's attention, for the same three reasons listed above that describe why callbacks work in comedy.

(1) A customer feels he's creating a story with you when you use callbacks, just the way an audience feels they are "in" on the joke each time a callback reappears.

(2) A callback adds continuity to your story, holding its pieces together and making it easier for the customer to understand the story.

(3) When you callback something your customer said previously, it shows the customer, unequivocally, that you have been listening to him. This is especially relevant when the idea you call back relates to something the customer said about himself or something that is important to him.

A callback is actually an effective gift for your customer, helping him make decisions, as in "You told me earlier that . . . " or "Last time when we met you showed me . . ." By referencing something earlier that is important to your customer, you make it easier for him to connect pieces of the conversation together, helping him sort through his issues.

Callbacks require alertness, squared

In discussing our Ditch the Pitch Habit, *Think input before output*, we focused on how *Being alert* can help an improvising actor or salesperson notice the details of a conversation.

Creating callbacks requires us to *Be alert* to what is happening right now, and simultaneously connect it to what happened previously. You can't plan for a callback, you need to notice when its opportunity arises, and jump on it. "A callback isn't forced," Charna Halpern explains. "But when the perfect time for a callback comes up, and you're present enough to realize it, you've got to grab it. The window of opportunity opens, and it closes pretty fast. If you're not present, you'll miss it." And, you need to notice the opportunity for a callback before anyone else. As Anne Libera of Second City adds, "If a callback is going to work, the audience shouldn't know it's coming right then. If they can see the callback coming a mile away, you don't get the laughter." Similarly, in a sales situation, well-placed callbacks make for productive surprises for your customer, creating "a-ha" connections that engage him deeper in the conversation.

So how do I incorporate callbacks into my persuasive conversations?

When creating persuasive conversations, I think of three steps that help me integrate callbacks into my conversations:

(1) Discover the opportunity for a callback

(2) Remember the opportunity for the callback

(3) Integrate the callback

The first step, discovering the callback, requires me to notice things that are important or interesting to my customer. A callback will have no value to the conversation if it has no value to the customer, so my first task is to discover the proper material for calling back. Continued references to the time I embarrassed myself in front of my entire third-grade class don't make for good callbacks if they are not interesting to my customer.

If you practice the other Ditch the Pitch Habits we've discussed so far in this book, you will inevitably discover good callback material. By *Thinking input before output* and *Sizing up the scene*, you will *Be alert* to what is important to your customer or to things that seem to capture her attention. After that, opportunities for callbacks will spontaneously spark in your mind.

One way I do this is by tracking the "Things That Matter" to my customer. For example, if, near the beginning of a conversation, my customer mentions a frustration that one of his products isn't selling as well as expected, I can assume that this is probably an important issue for him, and something worth referencing later. Likewise, if he had mentioned that sales are so strong that his company can't keep up with orders, and they are starting to upset their customers with poor service, I have now identified another opportunity for a callback.

In any persuasive conversation, assemble a mental list of the "Things That Matter" to your customer, and use these as fodder for callbacks.

Sometimes topics for callbacks have nothing to do with the specific content of your persuasive conversation. If a customer mentions his daughter's upcoming wedding, or the eagle he scored this past weekend on the toughest par 4 on the golf course, you may have found a good theme to recall into the conversation later.

The second step, remembering the callback, can be challenging for many people. After all, you are trying very hard to stay 100 percent engaged in the conversation, so it may be difficult to keep a running list of material to call back without distracting yourself.

I learned a helpful technique for remembering items that come up in a conversation from the book, *Moonwalking with Einstein, by* Joshua Foer, which describes how Foer went from forgetful twenty-something to U.S. Memory Champion in one year. Foer describes how "mental athletes," aka world-class memory experts, remember vast amounts of information. Foer explains that our brains evolved to remember spatial information particularly well, because survival for our ancestors depended on remembering where things were located. Which plant has the poisonous berries? Where do the tasty nuts grow? Where do the tigers like to hang out? To understand how well developed our spatial memory is, relative to other ways we remember information, imagine that two friends want you to know how their houses are laid out. The first friend shows you pictures of the rooms in his house and describes how the rooms are positioned. The second friend takes you on a walk through the actual house. Which would you be able to remember better?

In *Moonwalking with Einstein,* Joshua Foer describes how mental athletes take advantage of our amazing spatial memory capability by positioning things they need to remember inside mental pictures of places they know well. For example, if you need to remember a list of ten things to buy at the store, you could imagine each of these items positioned at various places throughout the home you grew up in. When you arrive at the grocery, all you would need to do is take a mental walk through your childhood home, encountering each item on the list as you walked through the front door, into the living room, kitchen, powder room, up the stairs, into the bedrooms, finally finding the Swiss chard you need to buy inside the pirate's chest in your childhood bedroom.[33]

You can do the same thing as you create a list of potential callbacks for use in a persuasive conversation with a customer. As opportunities for callbacks come up during a conversation, I try to associate a visual or spatial cue with the comment. For example, I recently sat with a potential client in his office to discuss a consulting project. As we talked he mentioned some key points that I wanted to remember. First he mentioned that he was interested in expanding into new geographic markets, so I pictured a globe on his credenza. A few minutes later he told me that he believes his salespeople could sell at higher prices, so I imagined a large dollar sign stuck on the window behind his desk. Additionally, I noticed a picture of him on the wall holding a large fish, and I made a note to refer to fishing later in the conversation. Each of these images provided a tool to help me remember these key points and call them back later in this conversation, and in future conversations.

The third step, integrating the callback, requires saintly patience and alertness. Patience is one of the most critical factors as you *ditch the pitch*. Pay attention, be alert, and when the opportunity to drop a callback into the conversation arrives, you will know. It will be natural. You will integrate the callback at the right time, because you are so focused on what is going on between you and your customer.

One thing to be careful about as you integrate a callback is to "play it cool." Don't be heavy handed and say, "Hey, look at me, aren't I clever? I just came up with a callback!" Avoid the circus performer's "Ta Dah!!!" Don't wait for the applause. Integrate the callback, and trust that your customer will notice it.

Callbacks can work over many timeframes. You can call back something your customer said ten minutes ago, or you can call back something she said last week. (She'll be impressed you remembered.)

In all cases, however, callbacks are one of the best ways to engage and impress a customer during persuasive conversations. She will feel like you are truly hearing her and that you really understand her. And, she will perceive continuity in the conversation that will make it much easier for her to remember your dialogue and integrate it into her purchase decision process.

> ### RECAP: Create Callbacks
>
> Always look for and use opportunities to call back information from earlier conversations or from earlier in this conversation, especially when you can reference something your customer said or that is important to your customer.

*   *   *

As we discussed earlier, the undeniable fact is that customers don't care that much about us. They care about themselves. The best way to get a customer to develop an interest in you is to weave elements of your story into your customer's story, creating a shared story.

This section described how to do that. First, *Focus the conversation on your customer,* not on what you are offering. Do this by ensuring that *95%* of the subject matter of your conversation is about your customer, by *Obeying the One-paragraph Rule* and by *Weaving your stories together.*

Next, *Don't rush the story.* If you *Avoid loading the slingshot,* are sure to *Leave things in your pocket* and *Create callbacks,* you will maintain the interest and engagement of your customer. As you continue to employ these practices, you will see a shared story emerge.

And, you'll notice how much more effective your persuasion is.

Part III

PUTTING DITCH THE PITCH TO WORK

Putting Ditch the Pitch to work is an all-day, everyday process. In this section we will address some key issues for integrating Ditch the Pitch Habits into your daily customer interactions. We will explore how to get a little bit better at *ditching the pitch* every day by practicing the Ditch the Pitch Habits. We will discuss how to turn conversations into business opportunities and persuading in groups. Finally, we will demonstrate how to use Ditch the Pitch principles to brainstorm new ideas.

These chapters will help you see ways to practice Ditch the Pitch Habits in many situations that you encounter every day.

The Dimmer Switch

7

Even if you are very skilled at *ditching the pitch*, you still have areas of potential improvement. If you are new to *ditching the pitch*, you are probably improving your skills every time you try. In either case, it is always possible to be better than you were, and it is always possible to be better than you are. Ditch the Pitch improvement happens in steps.

Learning to *ditch the pitch* is not like flipping a switch, where you immediately shift from novice to expert. Developing the Ditch the Pitch Habits happens gradually, much more like opening a dimmer switch than flipping an on/off switch. This is why even accomplished persuaders will continue to improve as they practice *ditching the pitch*; the dimmer switch can always go brighter. Your progress will accumulate as you get a little better at *ditching the pitch* every time you try. Don't focus on being perfect, focus on practice, and turn up the dimmer switch of improvement a bit at time.

ONE HABIT AT A TIME

To ensure this ongoing improvement, it's a good idea to focus on a few elements of the Ditch the Pitch principles at a time. Although I have presented the Ditch the Pitch Habits in a logical order, you do not have to work on them in that order. The habits are interdependent, mutually reinforcing each other. You eventually want to become fluent with all of them, but feel free to choose to work on the individual habits as you feel ready to do so, or as you feel the need to do so.

Below is the chart we use that summarizes the six Ditch the Pitch Habits, along with the eighteen practices that will help you learn these habits:

THE DITCH THE PITCH HABITS

Chapter 4: Figure Out What's Going On

HABIT #1
Think input before output

- Practice: Be alert
- Practice: Say less to notice more
- Practice: Turn down your analytic brain

HABIT #2
Size up the scene

- Practice: Know who you are with
- Practice: Understand the context of your conversation
- Practice: Listen for the game

Chapter 5: Go with the Flow

HABIT #3
Create a series of "yeses"

- Practice: Say, "Yes, and . . ."
- Practice: Work with what you are given
- Practice: Ensure your customer keeps saying yes

HABIT #4
Explore and heighten

- Practice: Find your customer's path
- Practice: Get rid of your but
- Practice: Make accidents work

Chapter 6: Let a Shared Story Emerge through Your Conversation

HABIT #5
Focus the conversation on your customer

- Practice: Make 95% of the conversation about your customer
- Practice: Obey the one-paragraph rule
- Practice: Weave your stories together

HABIT #6
Don't rush the story

- Practice: Don't load the slingshot
- Practice: Leave things in your pocket
- Practice: Create callbacks

Each of the conversations you have is an opportunity to improve your talents by *ditching the pitch*. In your next persuasive conversation, choose one of the six *Ditch the Pitch Habits* you want to improve, and focus on one of that habit's practices in that conversation. As you become more comfortable with that practice, work on that habit's other practices, one at a time. As you integrate multiple practices from one habit into a conversation, you will find that you are getting much more fluent with that habit.

For example, let's say that you have noticed that your customer conversations often lose steam, and you have a difficult time regaining conversational momentum when this happens. To address this issue, you decide to work on the Ditch the Pitch Habit *Explore and heighten*.

Explore and heighten is all about taking conversations to a higher level, engaging you and your customer in a more compelling, more interesting, more productive discussion. This habit has three practices:

(1) *Find your customers path* (page 86)

(2) *Get rid of your "but"* (page 91)

(3) *Make accidents work* (page 92)

Start by working on the practice *Find your customer's path*. This practice, as described on pages 86-90, recognizes that a productive conversation can only develop out of a flowing conversation, and it is easier to engage a customer if you don't force the conversation's direction. At the start of the conversation, let your customer set the direction, pace, and tenor of the conversation. This will make it easier to get you and your customer in a conversational flow together.

As you practice this, over and over again, there are a few pitfalls that you will want to avoid:

- Don't insist on starting at what you see as "the beginning" of the conversation. Be willing to start in the middle of the conversation; once you are flowing together it will be easier for you to move you and your customer to the topic of conversation you want to discuss.

- Resist the temptation to pull your customer onto your path in order to get the two of you in a conversational flow. The flow comes first, then the direction.

- Be patient. Even if your scheduled meeting is half over, and your customer is still telling you about his fishing trip, don't despair. At least he is engaged while he is telling you about his trip! Don't spoil this engagement, because if you keep his attention you will need less time to persuade him when the time comes.

Next, begin working on the practice *Get rid of your but*. Your customer will undoubtedly, say things that you do not agree with and/or that you do not want him to say. The natural, human reflex in these situations is to use the word "but."

Practice banishing the word "but" from your persuasive conversations, as described on page 91. This will seem difficult at first, but you will over time develop ways of subtly disagreeing with your customer without using the conversation-stopper, "but." You will notice your "but" usage will shrink, day to day.

As you become more fluent in *Finding your customer's path* and *Getting rid of your but,* begin working on the practice *Make accidents work*. As I have explained once an unexpected occurrence happens, there is nothing you can do about it, and you have to accept it as the new reality. Keep the principle that every idea is a bridge to the best idea in mind as you embrace unexpected occurrences and make them work.

As you employ these practices you will notice that your ability to *Explore and heighten* is improving, and that you are having an easier time keeping a customer engaged in a conversation and, more importantly, taking the conversation to a higher level.

Keep working on this habit—you will always be able to continue improving—and then choose another habit on which to focus. Maybe you will want to focus next on the first habit, *Think input before output,* or the habit *Focus the conversation on your customer.* As I mentioned above, you do not need to work on the habits in any special order, because they all work interdependently, and you will eventually employ them all concurrently.

STAYING FRESH

> *A lot of people start to study improvisation, knowing that it's about speaking without having any idea of what you're going to say. But then they begin to develop a repertoire of characters and repertoire of lines that those characters use, like a bucket of tricks. So when they improvise, they're actually drawing upon a reservoir of characters they've created, maybe five to ten. So it becomes another process, even within the world of improvisation, to teach people that it's not about creating a repertoire of script or a repertoire of characters. It's about creating the ability to develop an infinite amount of characters and an infinite amount of words.*
>
> —MICK NAPIER

Mick Napier's comment about improv actors developing their "bucket of tricks" can apply directly to salespeople, or anyone else who has to persuade others as part of their work. As you learn to *ditch the pitch*, you will inevitably find things that work. You may discover a particularly effective way to describe your offering to customers, or you may create a joke or story that succeeds in getting customers' attention. Be careful! It will be tempting to stash these successful techniques in your mental inventory and pull them out time and again. When you do this, you are pitching in pieces.

Consider for a moment what makes a particular explanation, joke, or story effective. Is it dependent on the exact words that you used? Is it possible to say it just as effectively with different words?

Of course it is possible to use different words. I'm 100 percent certain that you can take anything that you regularly say to customers and rephrase it, without losing any effectiveness.

Robert De Niro, Meryl Streep, and other expert actors are capable of delivering scripted lines in a way that sounds fresh and spontaneous. But most of us aren't De Niro or Streep. It's hard for us to sound fresh if we recite something that was written ahead of time. Much like listening to second-graders delivering their Christmas pageant lines in a singsong pattern, it's easy for our customers to detect when we've slipped into a scripted pitch.

Rehashed sentences, and many phrases shorter than a sentence, can sound to a listener like a "chunk of pitch." Pay attention when you hear people talking in social or business situations, and you can easily notice when people are regurgitating phrases, sentences, paragraphs, and stories that they've said verbatim many times before.

As you develop your Ditch the Pitch fluency, resist at all times the temptation to say anything as long as a sentence the same way twice. Rephrase it. Reword it. Recast it. Rewrite it. Redo it. There are many ways to say the same thing.

8

The Relationship Conversation: "Let's talk about us."

SCENE: You are at your friend's daughter's wedding, sitting next to someone you've never met before. You carry on a conversation over the course of the evening, and during that time he shares much information about his business. It becomes clear to both of you that this person could really use your professional help. You're *ditching the pitch*, practicing all of the habits we've learned so far in this book. At one point he says, "So how can you help me? Can we do some work together?"

In essence, he has asked, "Let's talk about *us*."

In dating relationships, this statement is often seen as either a welcome opportunity to move a relationship forward, or as a frightening ultimatum for someone who is not ready to commit. In an evolving business relationship, you hope your customer sees it as the former, not the latter. As a persuasive conversation develops with a prospective customer, you want this person to begin to see the possibility of a relationship with you; the challenge is how to make that happen.

Ideally, you would like your customer to bring up "the relationship conversation," as in the scenario above. Naturally, it is more effective for you if your customer asks how you can work together. However, there is only so long you can wait. If he doesn't start talking about a relationship, you will need to find the right way to do so yourself.

Let's explore the different ways a relationship conversation can begin.

LEADING YOUR CUSTOMER TO THE BRINK OF THE RELATIONSHIP

The best way to encourage a potential customer to start a relationship conversation with you is by weaving your customer's and your stories together, as described in the practice *Weave your stories together,* found on page 110. For many prospective customers, this will encourage them to start thinking "we" and they will eventually say, "Let's talk about us."

As you weave your stories together, your goal is for your customer to see her needs and interests intertwined with your capabilities. This will help your customer visualize the two of you working together and could prompt her to start a relationship conversation. Essentially what you are doing is bringing your customer to the "brink of the relationship," where she will hopefully say, "Let's talk about us."

But What If She Doesn't Start a Relationship Conversation?

As we've all experienced, life, especially with customers, is far from perfect. Even though a customer "should" start a relationship conversation with you, she may not. In these cases you need to take matters into your own hands and introduce the idea of creating a working relationship.

If you have been effectively weaving your stories together, your customer should be having thoughts about working with you, even if she hasn't mentioned it. If this is true, your role in bringing up a relationship conversation is to "confirm" something she is already thinking.

What is it she is already thinking? Well, if she is thinking about working with you, you can rest assured that she is *not* thinking about the depth of your product line or that you've "been in business since 1987," i.e., the kind of things that are (unfortunately) found on company websites or in company brochures. No, she is not thinking about you. She is thinking about how she could benefit by working with you.

Therefore, if you introduce a relationship conversation, you will most likely be successful if you frame the idea of a relationship in terms of how it could benefit her. You want to avoid (like the plague) anything that seems self-serving to you, such as the old-line sales stand-by, "I will do anything to earn your business." Why does she care that you really want her business? She cares only about how she will benefit by doing business with you.

Lead into the relationship conversation by focusing her attention on an improved future state that would occur if you worked together:

> *"Nicki, you've told me that you would have much stronger sales in your retail stores if your employees did a better job stocking and organizing the shelves, so customers could find the products they want. Imagine walking into one of your stores, six months from now, and the shelves look great. What would be different about that store's sales performance?"*

I call this technique "bringing the future forward." By helping Nicki envision a time in the future where her problem is fixed, you are helping her feel, in a tangible way, how valuable it would be to her to fix her problem. Most likely, Nicki will answer you by saying something to the effect of:

> *"I'm convinced that this problem is costing us 5 to 10 percent in sales, so I think that store would be doing at least 5 percent better. That's enough to make a significant difference at the bottom line, since the last 5 percent we sell in a store is very profitable."*

Now, you can introduce the idea of a working relationship by showing her how you can help her realize this improved future state:

"Nicki, with the right type of training program that includes ongoing reinforcement and reminders, your employees could be doing the things you want them to do, in a much shorter time-frame than six months. I can help you make that happen. Can we discuss how I could do that for you?

Note the use of the one-paragraph rule, and that you avoid *loading the slingshot* by bombarding Nicki with too many details about your ideas for helping her. This is a delicate part of your persuasive conversation, and it is critical that you continue to *ditch the pitch* and keep employing the disciplines, habits, and improvisation lessons you have learned. Don't start pitching now!

From this point, continue to *Figure out what's going on* (e.g., how well is she accepting the idea of working with you and what aspects of it seem to resonate with her), to *Go with the flow* (e.g., find mutual agreement and *Explore and heighten*), and to *Let a shared story emerge through your conversation* (this is a very important time to keep weaving your stories together).

But What If She Resists Your Attempt at a Relationship Conversation?

Well, then maybe the timing isn't right. Or maybe it's best to cut your losses and stop trying to pursue this customer. Not everyone can be your customer. Not everyone *should* be your customer. Your challenge, if this happens, is to determine if there is still a chance (that is worth pursuing) to create a relationship with this customer, or if you should move on to your next opportunity.

RELATIONSHIP CONVERSATIONS
IN NON-SALES SITUATIONS

The principle of the relationship conversation applies in persuasive situations other than selling to a new customer. For example, imagine that you need to persuade a person in another division of your company to cooperate and collaborate with you on a project. Just as it would happen in a selling situation with a prospective customer, your persuasion will be much more successful once the person from another division thinks "we" instead of "us and them." Your goal is for this person's frame of reference to focus on his relationship with you and not on the request you are making of him. In this regard, the situation is exactly like that with the prospective customer outlined above, and you can use the same techniques to create a relationship conversation.

As with all the Ditch the Pitch Habits, you will find that, with practice, you will become much more effective at creating relationship conversations, improving your overall ability to persuade.

9

The Persuasion Ensemble: Selling Together

One day early in my career, when I was director of marketing for vacation wholesaler MTI Vacations, I received a sales call from two people working for Chicago's local NBC affiliate, WMAQ. After greeting them in the lobby, I led them back to my office where they occupied the two seats on the other side of my desk facing me.

I was twenty-seven years old, and had never thought much about the art of the sales call. However, something seemed utterly wrong with the way these two guys handled the meeting. One of them would tell me something about their new advertising program, and then as soon as the first speaker left a small opening in his pitch, the other person would jump in with something he thought was more important. As they alternated back and forth, I began to notice that they were competing with each other to see who could tell more of his own version of their story. I, not surprisingly, became more aware of their competition than I was of their message. They both lost the competition.

Contrast this with a regularly-scheduled Monday night performance of "The Armando Diaz Experience" at Chicago's iO Theater. Ten or twelve performers, in a cast that varies week to week, will string together a one-hour performance with no previous discussion about plot, script, character, or which actor will take a lead role. As improvised scenes unfold, actors flow on and off stage, making room for each other and building on what others have said in previous scenes. They devote their complete attention to what is happening, even when they are not on stage, so that their personal work can blend with that of the ensemble.

It's impressive to watch people who are able to coordinate complex work. A double-play combination in major league baseball, a quarterback and receiver completing a pass by weaving a complex route through a dense defense, or jazz musicians working in a smoky club. All these instances require a fluid coordination between people. And each of them is improvised.

The musical group The String Cheese Incident came to prominence in the early 1990s, after playing music at ski resorts in Colorado. Twenty years later, the band has amassed a strong following as one of today's top jam bands, which implies that their songs contain a significant amount of group improvisation. I asked Michael Kang, who plays violin and electric mandolin for The String Cheese Incident, to describe how the six musicians in his band are able to improvise so fluidly as a group. "Music has to do with listening, reacting and conversing. When it's working, it's clear that we all feel the same way about what's happening. Then we achieve 'group lift-off.'"[34]

"Group lift-off." That's a great image. Do you achieve group lift-off when you and your colleagues persuade as a team?

Obviously, the NBC salespeople trying to pitch twenty-seven-year-old Steve couldn't achieve group lift-off. Imagine if, instead of competing with each other with their personal pre-written scripts, each had listened intently to what I was saying and to what his partner was saying, basing his comments only on what was relevant to the conversation at any given point in time. Michael Kang adds that improvisation is "an in-the-moment reaction to a group conversation. We listen, react, and converse." Imagine if, instead of coming into the meeting with their own pre-written scripts, the WMAQ salespeople had come in listening, reacting, and conversing—"jamming" like The String Cheese Incident. Imagine if they had coordinated their work, *ditched the pitch*, and created a fresh, spontaneous, meaningful persuasive conversation with me. I may have bought some ads from them.

Let's explore how to *ditch the pitch* as a group.

Think of yourselves as a "persuasion" ensemble." If you hear a rock band or a jazz ensemble, you don't notice only the music of the individual players. You notice and perceive the music of the entire group. The blend of their collective music-making creates your experience as a listener. Similarly, if you and one or more of your colleagues are persuading a customer, the customer isn't only influenced by each of you individually. Together, you and your colleague are perceived as an ensemble.

How can you become a "persuasion ensemble?"

Be conscious of the collective conversation you are having with your customer and of the collective experience you create with your customer. Don't think "Joe and I are on a sales call together." Think "Joe and I are creating a persuasive conversation with our customer." Think ensemble. Achieve "group lift-off."

Charna Halpern, the founder of iO, gives us an insight into how groups of improv actors at her theater create tight-knit improvisations. "One of the secrets to our large-ensemble improv at iO is that we treat each other as if we were geniuses, poets and artists."

Trust is such an overused word in business that it's easy to lose sight of what trust can mean in a specific business situation. When you are in a selling ensemble with colleagues you must have the kind of trust that a talented group of geniuses, poets, and artists would have. Or that a group of talented jazz musicians would have. You must have the utmost confidence that each thing one of your colleagues says or does in a selling situation is wonderful and important.

> *We treat each other as if we were geniuses, poets and artists.*
>
> —CHARNA HALPERN

TRY NOT TO TOP THE OTHER PERSON

The most obvious thing the two WMAQ salespeople did wrong was that they tried to compete with each other. A customer will immediately spot any competition between members of a persuasion ensemble. If you get irritated about what one of your colleagues says or does when you are working together in a persuasive situation, don't let your customer see your irritation. Acknowledge your partner, go with what he says, and gently work the conversation back to where you want it.

As we learned earlier, every idea is a bridge to the best idea. No matter where you are, "you can get there from here." Your colleagues' statements and actions become the new reality, and you must *Work with what you are given* in order to collaborate as a persuasion ensemble and accomplish your goals.

SHARED UNDERSTANDING OF THE PRINCIPLES

Good jazz players or improv actors can walk onto a stage with performers they have never met and successfully improvise. How do they do this?

In the case of the jazz players, they are able to improvise with strangers because each of the musicians is familiar with a tradition of jazz principles and idioms, a repertoire of standard tunes, and a willingness to obey the fundamental principles of improvisation, such as listening and saying "yes" to whatever your stage partners present to you. In the case of the improv actors, the actors meeting for the first time on the stage are familiar with the fundamental principles of improvisation and they are willing to use those principles to ensure a smooth scene.

To create a successful persuasion ensemble you need to ensure that each of you shares an understanding of and a respect for all the Ditch the Pitch Habits. Similar to a jazz or improv ensemble, your group will be able to create fresh, spontaneous, engaging experiences for your customers.

GIVE AND TAKE FOCUS

The give and take of focus is the "underlying structure of every scene,"[35] according to *The Second City Almanac of Improvisation*. At one moment the focus is on one character, the next moment it is on another. The way this focus transitions from one character to another sets the flow and rhythm of the scene, and, moreover, communicates much of the scene's meaning. Great film editors and directors use the change of focus between characters to great effect when composing a scene. Try to notice this the next time you watch a good movie.

Similarly, the actual flow of focus between different members of your persuasion ensemble and the customer gives your sales conversation its underlying structure. By allowing the focus to change gracefully from one member of your sales team to another and then to the customer (which could, of course, include more than one person), you will give the conversation character and personality. It will be much more interesting to your customer, the same way a movie is made interesting by the way focus shifts from character to character.

A natural give and take of focus within a persuasion ensemble is very difficult to achieve. If you seem like you are trying to one-up each other, as the WMAQ salespeople were doing, you will lose the respect and attention of your customer. On the other hand, if the customer sees the give and take of focus as a process through which you agree with each other and build on what each other says, you will draw the customer ever deeper into the conversation.

Sticking to the *One-Paragraph Rule*, described on page 106, is critical in an ensemble selling situation. Each one of you has to be careful not to monopolize the conversation, and always has to leave room for the other members of the selling ensemble (and, of course, the customer) to speak.

Earlier I described how ten or more improv actors can do a long scene and never once interrupt each other. The most obvious reason improv actors don't interrupt each other is that they are intently listening to what each other is saying, and are completely aware of what is happening around them. Watch people interrupt each other in a traditional business meeting, and you will clearly see people who aren't really paying attention to what others are saying, but are only looking for a small crack in the conversation into which they can insert a prepared comment they have been waiting impatiently to deliver. Awareness and acute listening are critical to a smooth give and take of focus, without interruption.

Creating a persuasion ensemble isn't really that hard, as long as you treat each other as geniuses, poets, and artists who fluidly give and take focus to create spontaneous persuasive conversations together.

10

Ditch the Pitch
to Brainstorm Ideas

*When we have a group of writers together coming up with ideas,
and someone says something silly, we never say, "that's dumb."
We laugh, because that dumb idea is going to lead to a great idea.*

—Charna Halpern

Although The Second City is the place where the high art of stage improvisation first developed, and where amazing improvisation can still be seen most every night of the week, some of Second City's most successful, well-attended, well-reviewed shows are "sketch" shows. Sketch comedy consists of a series of skits that, while they may vary a bit in each performance, are scripted. But, let's remember: this is still Second City, and so these scripts don't come into being in the typical way that most scripts do.

Anne Libera, who has also directed many Second City shows, describes the process like this: "We brainstorm and play in a safe place. And then we look at it and ask, 'What works best? Why does it work best?' And we're absolutely free to follow the ideas because if it doesn't work, that's fine. We won't do it again."

I spoke with Matt Hovde of Second City a few days after I saw a Second City sketch show he directed called *Spoiler Alert: Everyone Dies.* "In the show you saw on Sunday night the first two acts were scripted material. In other words, they weren't changing the lines every night and they knew exactly what the scenes were. But it took us two months to get to that scripted material, because in those two months they improvised the scene countless times. Sometimes they made a decision about what the story of the scene was going to be, and then they improvised ways to tell that story until they found a way that works."

Also in the true spirit of improvisation, a sketch show born from improvisation still has many opportunities to grow. "If you come to the same show a month later," Matt Hovde adds, "you'll see that it has changed. We are always improvising new ways to improve our shows."

There is much we can learn from these lessons about brainstorming freely and without judgment. Though we do not want to prepare a fixed sales pitch before a meeting with a customer, we can use the principles of improvisation to prepare for a persuasive conversation, exploring the best approach to take with that customer. We can play. We can experiment. We can explore. We can try things without the fear of failure.

At Yastrow & Company we use a similar process to develop strategies for dealing with particular clients. Through a process of role-playing we simulate a persuasive conversation with a client by first summarizing what we know about this client—his or her business issues, likes, dislikes, biases, past comments, personality quirks, etc. Then one of my team plays the client and we improvise a persuasive conversation together. The goal isn't just to prepare for a particular meeting, but to help us brainstorm and develop our overall approach for interacting with this customer. And, in the spirit of the way a Second City sketch show is written, we formulate our ideas through a process of improvisational trial and error, *Exploring and heightening, Saying "yes, and . . ."* and then ruthlessly editing. The main difference between this approach and a Second City sketch show is that we don't end up with a script. We use improvisation to brainstorm and develop our persuasive strategy for a given customer, without creating a fixed sales pitch for that customer. This improvisational preparation helps me *ditch the pitch* when I ultimately meet with the customer.

Go Ahead.
Ditch the Pitch.

11

Allow me to get personal for a minute.

This book took me much longer to write than my previous two books. The reason? I didn't just write this book. I lived it.

I started learning to *ditch the pitch* a number of years ago, and many of the ideas presented here were foreshadowed in my book *We: The Ideal Customer Relationship*. I spent a lot of time over the past three years refining what it means to *ditch the pitch,* and on improving my *ditch the pitch* abilities. In that time I have had hundreds of persuasive conversations, constantly monitoring my progress. I have interviewed many talented improv actors and improvising musicians, and took two improv courses at Second City. I've been thoroughly immersed in the idea of improvisation. During this process I have spent many evenings in my basement music studio, translating the concepts presented in this book to my ability to improvise on guitar.

The result is that I have developed the tools to improvise in conversations with customers and have become much more effective at engaging them in persuasive conversations.

I'm convinced that anyone can learn to *ditch the pitch,* and that the ideas in this book can help people persuade more effectively, no matter what their jobs are. Work toward making these habits second nature, and you will transform your ability to engage and persuade customers.

Go ahead. Ditch the pitch.

Acknowledgments

Of all of my books, *Ditch the Pitch* was certainly the most fun to write. I spent hours talking to actors, musicians and business people about how they improvise, and why it is important. What's to complain about when that's what's keeping you busy?

It goes without saying that a project like *Ditch the Pitch* requires the help of many people.

My wife Arna has been, is, and will always be my most influential editorial voice. She was working as a professional editor when I met her, and her years of experience as a teacher have only honed her critical skills. More importantly, it's a lot of fun discussing my work with her.

Members of my team at Yastrow & Company also provided invaluable help. Heather Blonsky immersed herself in this book, and it would not be what it is without her. Heather's fingerprints are all over *Ditch the Pitch*. Caroline Ceisel brought her enthusiasm and skills for improvisation into the early, formative stages of this project. Amanda Cullen, Joanne Glass, and Helga Gruenbauer, my other associates at Yastrow & Company, played key, unique roles in helping me progress from early ideas to a published book.

I always rely on my family as sounding boards and brainstorming partners, and my dad Shelby, mom Sybil, sister Sara, brother Phil, and daughter Nurit all gave important feedback. I am fortunate that my two sons, Levi and Noah, regularly play music with me, and I have spent many hours improvising with both of them. That's a real treat. My aunt, Roslyn Grodzin Alexander, gave me great insights from her renowned work as an actress, contributing to *Ditch the Pitch* as she did to my previous book, *We: The Ideal Customer Relationship*. My ongoing conversations with my cousin Neal Kusnetz have shaped all three of my books.

I am also fortunate to have a number of friends with whom I continually discuss ideas: Karyn Kedar, Ezra, Chuck Rosenberg, Rachel Rosenberg, David Gottlieb, David Baker, Franklin Drob, and Brian Kovach. Thanks to each of you for our many rich conversations about ditching the pitch.

The team at SelectBooks, Kenzi Sugihara, Kenichi Sugihara, and Nancy Sugihara were, as with my previous books, perfect partners for this endeavor. Nancy's editing gave important final shape to the book. Cathy Mosca also gave me important advice and feedback, as she did with my previous book. Thanks to Janice Benight for the beautiful design of the pages in this book. Thanks also to Yvonne Nienstadt, Rich Sheridan, and Alex von Bidder for sharing their wisdom in this book.

I interviewed a number of important musical "giants" for this book, including Yossi Fine, John Moulder, Michael Kang and Douglas Ewart, all who inspire me greatly with their improvisational skills and insights. I have learned much from these people.

Also, since I live in the Chicago area, the "world capital" of stage improvisation, I had the chance to interview many improv actors and leaders of the Chicago improv scene, including Susan Messing, Mick Napier, Charna Halpern, Ann Libera, Matt Hovde, and Jessica Rogers. Tom Yorton and Steve Johnston of Second City Communications also provided invaluable guidance and feedback to me.

This book is dedicated to my uncle, Ed Yastrow, who died just as I was finishing the manuscript. My uncle was my teacher and, in addition to much concrete knowledge, I learned from Ed the joy of learning for learning's sake. His influence on me is permanent and indelible.

Endnotes

1   R.I.M. Dunbar. "Language, Music, and Laughter in Evolutionary Perspective." University Press Essays, 2007 Redwood Audiobooks. Accessed via Audible.

2   Steven Pinker. *The Language Instinct* (New York: W. Morrow and Co., 1994).

3   Tom Yorton. "Using Improv Methods to Overcome the Fear Factor." *Employment Relations Today* 31, Winter 2005: 8, doi: 10.1002/ert.20036.

4   Anne Libera, interview by author, conducted at The Second City, Chicago, IL, September 2011.
    All subsequent references to comments made by Anne Libera are from this interview.

5   Mick Napier, interview by author, conducted at The Annoyance Theater, Chicago, IL, March 2012.
    All subsequent references to comments made by Mick Napier are from this interview.

6   Frans de Waal. *Our Inner Ape: A Leading Primatologist Explains Why We Are Who We Are* (New York: Riverhead Books, 2005.)

7   Douglas Ewart, interview by author, conducted in Evanston, IL, June 2011.

8   John Moulder, interview by author, Chicago, IL, February 2013.

9   Tom Yorton. "Using Improv Methods to Overcome the Fear Factor," page 9.

10 Tom Yorton. "Overcoming Barriers to Innovation: Balancing Management and Creation." *Employment Relations Today* 32, 2005: 5, doi: 10.1002/ert.20081.

11 Yossi Fine, interview by author, Tel Aviv, Israel, April 2013.
    All subsequent references to comments made by Yossi Fine are from this interview.

12 Yorton, "Using Improv Methods to Overcome the Fear Factor," page 9.

13 Susan Messing, interview by author, Chicago, IL, May 2011.
    Unless otherwise noted, all subsequent references to comments made by Susan Messing are from this interview.

14 Jessica Rogers, interview by author, Chicago, IL, September 2011.

15 Yvonne Nienstadt, interview by author, Tecate, Mexico, January 2012.

16 Susan R. Glaser, and Peter A. Glaser. Be Quiet, Be Heard: *The Paradox of Persuasion* (Eugene, Or.: Communications Solutions, 2006).

17 Charles Limb. "Your Brain on Improv." Filmed November 2010. TED Talk. Posted January 2011. http://www.ted.com/talks/charles_limb_your_brain_on_improv.html.

18   Robert B. Cialdini. *Influence: The Psychology of Persuasion* (New York: Collins, 2007).

19   Alex von Bidder, telephone interview by author, January 2012, and personal conversations, Tecate, Mexico, February 2012.
All subsequent references to comments made by Alex von Bidder are from these interviews.

20   Anne Libera. *The Second City Almanac of Improvisation* (Evanston, IL: Northwestern University Press, 2004), page 105.

21   Susan Messing, interview by Elysabeth Alfano, *Fear No ART Chicago,* Annoyance Theater, Chicago, IL, July 2011.

22   Messing, *Fear No ART Chicago* interview.

23   Matt Hovde, interview by author, Chicago, IL, September, 2011.
All subsequent references to comments made by Matt Hovde are from this interview.

24   *The Second City Almanac of Improvisation,* page 160.

25   *The Second City Almanac of Improvisation,* page 33.

26   Alan Weiss—from speech given by Mr. Weiss, Warwick RI, December 2012.

27   *The Second City Almanac of Improvisation,* page 10.

28   Yorton, "Overcoming Barriers to Innovation: Balancing Management and Creation," page 5.

29   *The Second City Almanac of Improvisation,* page 11.

30   Yorton, "Using Improv Methods to Overcome the Fear Factor," page 12.

31   *The Second City Almanac of Improvisation,* page 104.

32   R.B van Baaren, et. al., University of Nijmegen in the Netherlands, published in the *Journal of Experimental Social Psychology* (39, 2003), pp. 393-398.

33   Joshua Foer. *Moonwalking with Einstein: The Art and Science of Remembering Everything* (New York: Penguin Press, 2011).

34   Michael Kang, telephone interview by author, March 2013.
All subsequent references to comments made by Michael Kang are from this interview.

35   *The Second City Almanac of Improvisation,* page 17.

Index

About the Author

photo by Chime Costello

In addition to *Ditch the Pitch*, Steve Yastrow is the author of *We: The Ideal Customer Relationship* and *Brand Harmony*. Steve is a former senior marketing executive with Hyatt Hotels and Resorts and the current president of Yastrow and Company, a Chicago-based consulting and advisory firm.

As a consultant, speaker, and writer, Steve helps people and organizations create powerful stories and communicate them in ways that build customer relationships and drive results. Steve's consulting clients include McDonald's Corporation, Kimpton Hotels & Restaurants, The Tom Peters Company, The Cayman Islands Department of Tourism, Jenny Craig International, and Great Clips for Hair, among many others.

Steve lives in Chicago, Illinois, with his wife Arna, where they raised their three children, Nurit, Levi, and Noah.

For more information on *Ditch the Pitch*,
please visit www.yastrow.com.